WINNING ANYWHERE

the *power* of

"SEE"

dibyendu de

THE N-E-M-E WAY

Winning Anywhere -
the Power of 'See'

Winning Anywhere - the Power of 'See'

The N-E-M-E Way

DIBYENDU DE

PARTRIDGE

A Penguin Random House Company

Copyright © 2014 by Dibyendu De.

Cover Design by Rick De

ISBN: Hardcover   978-1-4828-1841-3
               Softcover   978-1-4828-1840-6
               Ebook   978-1-4828-1839-0

All rights reserved. No part of this book may be used or reproduced by any means, graphic, electronic, or mechanical, including photocopying, recording, taping or by any information storage retrieval system without the written permission of the publisher except in the case of brief quotations embodied in critical articles and reviews.

Because of the dynamic nature of the Internet, any web addresses or links contained in this book may have changed since publication and may no longer be valid. The views expressed in this work are solely those of the author and do not necessarily reflect the views of the publisher, and the publisher hereby disclaims any responsibility for them.

To order additional copies of this book, contact
Partridge India
000 800 10062 62
www.partridgepublishing.com/india
orders.india@partridgepublishing.com

CONTENTS

Dedicated to

Dad, who was more than a father could ever be.
I failed to repay what I took from him; both the
substantial and the insubstantial

PREFACE

For little over three decades I have paid attention to a question that occupied my mind for long: 'Why humans fail?' This is just because no one likes 'failures' and everyone wants to win. So what is the secret of wining anywhere? I am not hinting at unethical ways of winning through stealing, manipulating, forcing others into submission and all that stuff. It was more a matter of how one can solve his own problems in life and that of others to live harmoniously and peacefully; the goal being how to develop one's potential to the highest possible level through whatever one is engaged in within the given constraints. Seen in another way, the question is how one can create his/her own destiny in our engineered world. More specifically, I wanted to find the single most important ability a person must have to negotiate life as it is but still do something about it to shape his destiny.

Fortunately, being an engineer, I was engaged with our engineered world right from the beginning of my professional career. Through machines, products, processes, systems, factories, organizations of various types and hues and through the behavior and movement of people, I saw the moving spirit of man and his determined effort to survive well. All of reality was projections of the collective human mind in some way or the other. If things failed, whether in work or personal life, it was the mind that failed. Or stated more explicitly, the human mind is constantly engaged with reality. Reality triggers our thoughts and emotions.

If that matches with the nuanced reality one is seeing it leads on to success in terms of happiness and joy of living. When our thoughts do not match reality, frustrations, sufferings and pain are caused. The primary reason for all failures is one's inability to understand reality or become aware of the total situation one is in. Having said that, failures, pain, frustration and suffering serve as starting points to develop awareness of the total situation one is faced with. Such failures act as signals. Or in Nemetic language acts as a type of 'exchange'. In a way it is welcome since failure is something which people notice easily and want to do something about it.

Moreover, failures linger in our minds much longer than successes, which are fleeting as one success is usually outdone very quickly by another. So in a way, we learn much more from our failures than from our successes only if we openly accept them as 'teachers'; opening up the greatest potential for 'learning well' and acting effectively with wisdom. It starts with the power of 'see'.

The book is presented in a special way. Keeping with the nature of complexity, each chapter, in a way, acts as a fractal of the whole. They are like holograms, each reflecting the whole. And like any complex adaptive system each chapter creatively interacts with other chapters since they are not only interdependent but also independent and like any good dialog that builds up on each interaction.

ACKNOWLEDGEMENTS

I am grateful to Michael Josefowicz who started the mantra of NEME (Notice, Engage, Mull and Exchange). Thereafter the whole discipline of Nemetics evolved over dialogs held on Twitter with many Twitter pals, most importantly D. C. Padhi, Dan R D and Sean Grainger.

Over the years Michael and I have been sparring partners in dialogues and application of Nemetics. He introduced to me his language of Nemetics waiting for real life applications. And I in turn slowly introduced to him my methods of solving 'complex' and 'wicked problems' waiting for a language to express the essence. Since then it has come a long way to its present state of development through constant practice that informed the theory. Till date, the discipline and practice of Nemetics are being developed through numerous conversations, applications to live problems and training and education programs all of which form significant part of the ongoing Action Research in the development of Nemetics. Such practical self organizing way of development of the discipline is what we call 'praxis' that informs our theory, which then goes on to develop the practice in an iterative manner.

There could not have been a better relationship that resonated at once fulfilling each other's mutual needs. I am grateful to Michael.

I am immensely grateful to D C Padhi. He has been a constant companion for the last three years in my journey and an avid practitioner of my methods, techniques and the 'way' on which he has unrelenting faith. He has constantly encouraged me to write this book and supported me throughout with his intense dialogs on each and every thought that appear in this book. Such friendship is invaluable.

I am also greatly indebted to organizations like Tata Metaliks Kobutu Pipes Limited, Tata Metaliks Limited, Tata Chemicals Limited, UltraTech, Vikram Cement, Grasim Cement, Tega Industries Limited, and Hindustan Unilever for providing opportunities and the playground where the action research of Nemetics (from 1990 till date) played out to resolve their complex issues and 'wicked problems' in manufacturing systems, design, human and learning systems.

However, I am immensely grateful to my Guru Tim Henry, of the University of Manchester, whose gentle voice coaxed me along on the 'not so friendly' roads of Condition Based Maintenance (respond accordingly to reality), Reliability, Design Improvements, Complexity and Chaos and to stay with that exciting journey, whenever tiredness overcame me. With his light I saw how all these seemingly diverse subjects are really entangled as one.

I am indebted to Dad, who spent countless hours at my study table from my young school days teaching me how to look at social systems in totality, their birth, development, death and reformation. It was and still is a pleasure listening to him explaining social movements and development. It not only shaped my young mind but also gave me the understanding that we as a 'human species' simply do too much and unnecessarily waste too much. There are easier ways. This book is dedicated to him.

But without the immense patience and tolerance exhibited by my wife, Madhumita, for putting up with my crazy emergent ways of passionately engaging with Nemetics, this book would not have seen the light of the day. I am grateful to her.

A sense of gratitude fills me for the immense support and constant encouragement provided by Partridge Publishers in taking the initiative to publish the book and exchanging the value it contains with many.

In a way, like all complex systems, each and every one of them left their entangled and hard to segregate, imprints on the development of this important subject, which only enriched the discipline through spontaneous co-evolution.

Zen koan, 'Walking on the sword's edge; Living in fire'.

Chapter 1

Sa of Mr. Giri

"The ability to shape a narrative of our lives by ourselves is the essence of human freedom. How many can do that?"—@predictswan

On the evening of 15th March 2013, Mr. Giri called me up. Mr. Giri is one of the middle level managers of an Indo-Japanese production unit in the state of West Bengal, India.

He was very happy and excited to announce, "you must know that we have broken all previous records of production."

"Is that so?" I asked; my voice laced with expectant excitement.

"Yes, it is true . . . almost unbelievable. We have shot up from producing 200 units per day to 2000 units per day from the same machines. Our quality rejection has dropped from 14% to around 5%. We have crossed the 8000 tons per month target . . ." he almost gasped for breath to continue, ". . . and I must thank you so much . . ."

Indeed, this was incredible! His company was struggling for the last five years to crank up production and make some profit to survive. They identified the bottleneck of the plant but were simply unable to do anything about it. Their Japanese partner introduced all their famous improvement tools and techniques they had in their arsenal. Everyone sweated and puffed and huffed but no improvement was forthcoming. All efforts were in vain. The Japanese management team blamed the Indians for their 'work attitude', 'lethargy', 'incompetence' and gross overall 'stupidity' . . . This obviously made the Indians angry. They in turn called the Japanese 'overbearing', 'conceited', 'racists', 'foolish' and what not . . . But at the end of the day in spite of all that shouting, mud-slinging and sledging no iota of improvement was in sight. In fact, things went for a nose dive. Crisis of closure loomed in the horizon as losses mounted.

"Thank me for what?" I asked with a tinge of eagerness.

Then he went on to tell me a story. "You know what the great Indian music maestro Tansen said?"

"No. I don't have a clue about what he said," I mumbled.

Giri continued with a tone mixed with excitement and reverence, "Tansen said if you only know how to sing the first note of seven notes (Sa, Re, Ga, Ma, Pa, Da, Ni, Sa) in music very well, you automatically get to sing all notes fluidly."

'Hmm . . .' I nodded in agreement. 'Right, but what has that to do with me?' I asked.

"Everything," he quipped back. "You taught us the first note so well that I have now learned to sing anything."

Absolutely clueless about what he actually meant I asked with curiosity getting better of me: "And what was that first note?" This was because I have tried to teach them many things to improve their performance over a period of 18 months.

"Oh, didn't you teach us how to pay attention or observe things and their connections in their own settings without seeing what the mind already knows?" He replied, bit incredulously.

"Yes, I remember that. And you think that was so important?" I pressed in to learn more from him.

"It was. And it would continue to be so for the rest of my life. It makes me so confident that I think I can **work and win anywhere in the world**, tackle anything in the world and solve any problem in the world," he said with a slow deliberate voice exuding lot of conviction.

"Thank you again and would you mind if I come over to Kolkata to meet you some day to learn more of what you say as **NOTICE**?" He seemed to stress the last word.

This was the first time in five years they made a decent profit that pulled them out of impending closure.

As the conversation ended, I sat on the sofa with waves of happiness sweeping over me. I thought to myself, OMG! The power of the humble **NOTICE** is just amazing! Nothing more is needed. We need not teach people how to think. They know how to think. We need not teach people so many tools and techniques. They would discover those by themselves. We simply don't need to waste their time doing things which we think must be done. We need not bore them to death to the point of getting disengaged. We simply need to teach those who really want to sing well the first note of the four notes (Notice, Engage, Mull, Exchange)—"**NOTICE**". The rest follows automatically. That's all!

I noticed my tea getting cold . . .

Chapter 2

Nemetics—an outline

"Reality triggers thoughts: Thoughts create reality"—
by @predictswan

That was Nemetics in brief. As you might have
already guessed by now the music of Nemetics
is made up of only four simple notes—
Notice, **E**ngage, **M**ull and **E**xchange (NEME).

The mantra NEME, explained in a simple way would
mean:—

Notice means 'seeing' with all our senses.

Engage means making sense of what we see.

Mull means to think through the products of the
'engage' to make intelligent choices for responding
to a situation.

Exchange is the actual process of responding to a
situation in a given context by various means.

But then one might ask, 'Don't people see? Aren't we
seeing all the time and make sense of what we see? Is
there a need to see or notice everything all the time?'

There is, however, a big difference, when we see things the Nemetics way.

We see with attention when faced with a problem, pain, suffering or intense feeling. In other cases our brain keeps watch on our surroundings without making us edgy. It is the previous case that we refer to in Nemetics.

A further explanation would be something like this:

In addition to seeing problems, pains, sufferings or intense feelings, we can of course see the world around us and Nature in diverse ways without the immediate pressure to come to, or rather jump to, any conclusion or interpretation? (Notice)

What if we hold all the diverse experiences of 'seeing' and interpret each view separately and in combination? (Engage)

What if we think through the products of 'Engage' and make intelligent choices of our various interpretations as per our limitations and given constraints? (Mull)

What if, given our choice we made, we design a response; most appropriate to the situation and exchange it with the world in form of communication, solutions or re-designs? (Exchange)

Why then Mr. Giri was so concerned about 'Notice', the first note? As we notice things other notes of the music, like Engage, Mull and Exchange follow automatically cascading like a water wave from one rock to the next till Notice is finally exchanged with others in some form.

Here is a stylized representation of the flow of Mr. Giri's music.

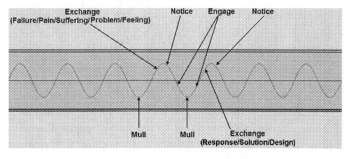

© Michael Josefowicz & Dibyendu De

Notice that there is no 'theory' or 'model' involved. There is no particular way of 'noticing'. Or in other words, we don't see the world only through a fixed theory or model, however attractive that might seem to be. That is not to say that theories and models are unhelpful or unproductive. But they are more useful in the 'Engage stage' rather than in the 'Notice stage'. A model would only prove to be useful, if it helps us understand reality better. We also do not proceed to exchange our responses through any fixed or predetermined step-by-step process.

Is there one way of seeing anything? Though the answer is deceptively simple, most try to ignore the obvious and try to see things in one particular way. A businessman would see the world in one particular way and no other way is acceptable to him. Similarly Capitalistic economies see the world in a specific manner. They are relentless about their way of seeing things in terms of expansion and growth even if they trample upon millions of lives and Nature. Same it is for Marxists. They even want art to reflect their ideology. But why should it be so?

For example, if we are viewing a simple window, there are many ways of seeing it.

We can see it as an opening that lets in fresh air when we feel stuffy inside a room.

We can also choose not to see too much of the window but the perhaps see and enjoy the excellent view of Nature that it might offer.

We can then see the connection between a window and the hygiene of a room. We can see it as a medium of exchange that lets in sunlight and fresh air and drives out bacteria and dust that accumulate in the room.

We may also see the state of economy and material prosperity of the neighborhood by paying attention to the quality of the window materials used and the way they are arranged and painted.

We can see a window as a window to the culture of the place like 'bay windows indicating 'surplus' of leisure; 'jafri' windows of Rajasthan as a means to protect privacy of women from unwanted gaze of strangers or the 'jali' windows of old Kolkata displaying aristocracy of the household.

We can look at a window to get an idea of the climate of a place. Hotter climate calls for smaller windows and use of less glass. Colder climates necessitate use of larger windows and glasses to trap the available heat of a weak sun.

We can also see many windows in the neighborhood to see whether the neighborhood belongs to working class community or to the privileged class.

We can with some patience wait to see the effect of traffic on the windows of our interest. Do they rattle with the vibration of a motor cycle passing by or by the blare of its horn? If they rattle a lot then we can be sure that the life of the window panes would be short enough forcing the owner to spend substantial money on its upkeep if he or she cares to keep the draught out on a chilly day in December.

There are so many ways to see reality! No doubt it would bring up diversity of views. But that is true of any reality. Reality of anything is made up of diverse views or 'sees'. Wisdom lies in accepting all views and living with them but choosing one or some according to one's intention, needs, limitations and constraints in a given context.

'Seeing' is the spiritual part of anything.

How is that?

Because in India spirituality is described in a very simple way—it is nothing but the power of paying attention with a still mind and being aware of the possibilities such viewing unfolds. The Sanskrit word for that is 'Darshan', which encompasses all forms of seeing and knowing.

If so, there is hardly any divide between spirituality and materialism because without the form, which materialism provides, there is no spirituality or nothing to notice or 'see.'

Similarly, there is also no divide between our inner world and the external world. The secrets of both worlds can only be revealed through the power of 'seeing' or paying attention by a still mind and becoming aware of all possibilities. Essentially then the divisions that we create between materialism and spirituality and between our inner world and the external world are all in the mind, which stops us from seeing anything as an indivisible whole. There seems to be no harm in classification if only we remember that every division that we make only reflects the others.

After 'see' all that is left for us to do then is rather straightforward and easy. We are then left to engage with the possibilities that compete for further attention in our awareness space and carefully choose (mull) the ones that satisfy a given need in a given context within its existing limitations and then exchange the choice with others. It also means that we have a choice of 'notice not' the other choices for the moment. However, whether the exchange improves the life of the individual and/or that of others would depend on the intention of the 'seer.'

For instance, decades back when I lived and studied in the UK I was struck by the almost staggering beauty of the rolling green fenced farmlands stretching over miles. There wasn't much to see save landscaped manicured grass tops with herds of sheep grazing lazily without a sheep dog in sight.

What am I to make of this sight?

If I were an artist I would have been possibly thrilled at seeing such a beautiful landscape to paint. I would have enjoyed doing that.

If I were a sociologist then I would have seen something else. I would have seen how land laborers have handed over their strips of land to the richer gentry and moved to the cities to eke out an earning. And I would have also 'seen' that such mass migration to the cities had had taken place at least one generation earlier, if not more. If I see that I would also see that major cities of the UK are less likely to face the global problem of 'arrival cities' faced by other cities like Shanghai, Mumbai or Rio.

Had I been a student of political economy I would have seen the changes in social hierarchies, money flow, relationship between the present landed gentry and the landless and changes in the social infrastructures to support present means of livelihood.

However, if I were an ecologist, I would be seeing more of the changes in the ecology that might have taken place when people moved from their ancestral farmlands.

Or suppose I were an agricultural scientist I would perhaps immediately set out to see the difficulty present farm owners might face in creating sufficient organic fertilizers for the grass to stay greener and sheep to remain healthier.

So seeing would be many of such things, such as:—

1. Seeing depends on intentions. Intentions inform what one sees and acts upon.
2. Seeing the visible and the invisible.
3. Seeing the relationships between different visible and invisible 'objects.'
4. Seeing the 'sayable' and the 'unsayable'.
5. Seeing needs, limitations & constraints of a particular situation.
6. Seeing changes that have happened or are going to happen soon.
7. Seeing the past, present and the future in the 'long now' (that is in the present).
8. Seeing as a way to learn and create new knowledge.
9. Seeing of reality may be done in so many different ways. All ways are valid.

Perhaps a word or two on 'intentions' to clarify what it is all about, would now be in place before we go any further.

Chapter 3

Intention is the difference that creates the difference in seeing

"@ddrrnt pure intention is only paying attention to capture reality & not impose any thot on reality @toughLoveforx @johnkellden @graingered" by @predictswan

Intention is the difference that creates the difference in how we see things differently leading to different actions.

Even, as it often happens, same information or data or a trend chart creates two different meanings for two persons seeing the same information at the same time. Their intentions differ.

Same object, reality, scenario or information creates two different meanings for a person over a period of time. This is because the intention towards the information changes over time. Therefore difference is created.

Same poem can evoke two different responses from two different personas. The intention makes the difference in interpretation.

Two persons speak the same sentence in two different ways. Intention makes the difference. The tone, the pitch and loudness give away the intention, which can be seen.

Same lecture is understood in two different ways by two students. Their intention towards the lecture, lecturer, content and subject differs. And that creates the difference.

A student says, 'I am not able to memorize anything. I must first understand something very well before it gets under my skin." It is her intention that would determine whether she would remember or fail to remember or remember after a lot of struggle and time.

Plain looking Jack loves a plain looking Jane. A plain looking Jane suddenly turns into a beautiful princess in the eyes of a plain looking Jack and not to other Jacks. They are suddenly transformed into a Cinderella or a Hamlet. Their intention towards each other made the difference in the way they see each other.

One single photo posted on Facebook generates 31 different comments. It is the intention of a commentator towards the photograph; photographer and other commentators that creates the difference in the way each commentator sees the same picture. Their intentions that create the difference are out in the open for others to feel. Palpable!

People enter a 'brain-storming' session already knowing what the management wants of them to see, hear and tell and they storm their brains or think accordingly. The output of such meetings is determined by the intention of the management. If the management's intention is to force people to buy-in something people would buy in. If the management's intention is to create an open creative environment to foster creativity and innovation then the output would be creative solutions and innovation. The intention of the management creates the difference in the outcome.

No one can possibly sell anything to anyone unless the intention of the buyer allows for that. Sales figures of different regions differ by the intention of the customers from different regions depending on how they see the product, service or the experience.

A win or a loss of a political party in any democratic election is a result of voters' intention. Pubic intention makes the difference between a winner and a loser in fair democratic politics.

Intentions create memories. Intentions create actions. Intentions create results. Intention creates beauty. Intention creates chaos and complexity. But most importantly, intentions inform what we want to see or don't want to see.

Clearly, intention is a highly emotional response. It may or may not be subjected to rational thinking, rationale, logic, or this theory or that. It is created from direct experience or direct perception of a person or influenced by others whom one trusts and respects. It is influenced by the state of the environment (physical, mental, spiritual) one lives. It can't be influenced or modified or changed by force or being battered by mantras, dogmas and rituals. It is sudden. It is emergent. It is chaotic.

Intention is also the glue that binds **collaborative** efforts.

Intention paves the way for a heart to heart dialog to create meaning and evolve into higher **consciousness**.

Intention creates trust and **love** between two persons.

Intention creates the **environment** that determines whether an employee would give out his/her heart for the work or leave an organization.

Intention creates the **relationship** between the teacher and her students helping a student to love and master a subject.

Intention helps us **find** things and be happy about it.

Intention helps us link two distinct memories, words, thoughts, ideas, images, solutions, people into something more than any one of the original items. Intention is the source of **emotions, which are linked to what we see**. Intentions might also augment memory preventing us from seeing what should be seen. Intentions can also block right perception and cognition or trigger cascades of emotions and cognition, which may or may not help us 'see' things.

Intention creates a brilliant **business** or a failed one.

Intention helps us achieve seemingly **impossible** tasks.

Intention restores our **health** or destroys it.

Intention would determine whether a **problem** would be solved or would it remain unsolved.

It would also determine the consequences of a **decision**.

Intentions can be **felt** or understood even in silence, without a word passing between persons.

Intention determines whether one would express (exchange) what one sees or learns in the form of poems, prose, mathematics, scientific rationale, speech, art, story, . . . etc.

In others words intention is the cornerstone of personal development and creative leadership.

In simple terms, intention is, **"What do you want?"**

Those simple words must be the first words of a leader to his/her followers.

Are we clear about what we want?

Have we made it clear?

It hardly matters whether it is explicit or implicit. But it has to be there. Once there, the rest happens automatically and **effortlessly**.

It is the difference that creates all the differences in the way we view anything.

Intention works like magic to create the differences that we see around us. There would never be a world where everybody thinks and behaves alike or can be forced to think or behave alike. It is foolish to expect that to happen. That is the fundamental diversity we must all accept if we are to go forward in our human journey in a harmonious and creative way. For creative flow to happen between two persons or within a group, acceptance of such diversity of 'seeing' the same is a must. Then only creativity flows.

However, the preferred intention at the 'Notice' stage is a 'no-mind' state to unravel potentiality and possibilities in what we see. Else the outcome might be grossly skewed.

The Important Question—What do you want?

Imagine leadership that would inspire thousands of landowners to freely give up millions of acres of their land to those who needed it. This was the Bhoodan Land Gift Movement in India in the 1950s—the largest voluntary transfer of land in human history.

It began with the simple question posed to a village gathering by Vinoba Bhave, a follower of Gandhi:

"What do you need?" An answer and solution emerged from the group and then spread organically, as Bhave and thousands of others walked through every district in India. Without any government involvement, they transferred millions of acres of land to the most impoverished villagers, so they could grow their own food.

Embedded in this dramatic example of non-violent change is a new vision of leadership. This was not a top-down command and control leadership, but one that arose in many individuals and groups as the process unfolded.

This leadership began with asking and listening. It was open to the solutions that emerged and adapted them to work within the complex social and governmental systems.

This is an example of what we call whole systems leadership, where leadership emerges against a problem.

Tough problems need a different way of solving them—observing, viewing it in the right perspective, questioning, open way of talking, listening, doing and allowing and accepting new realities to emerge.

A Koan:

A monk asked Master Yun-men: "What is the fundamental teaching in life?"

Yun-men: "No question, no answer."

Chapter 4

Seeing the future in the long now

"@toughLoveforx If we haven't noticed, there is no reality since reality only reflects of our consciousness"— by @predictswan

Prof. Md. Yunush, the founder of Grameen Bank has something remarkable to share on seeing the 'big picture.'

He said that as an economist he always saw the big picture of everything. He could see how things would change and how things fitted into one another. And if something was done how that something would affect the big picture. But after that 'big picture' seeing and thinking he could not do anything worthwhile or bring about any significant change anywhere or solve any nagging problem.

Till one day he saw the misery and pain of 42 families ravaged by a cruel flood. When he chose to see more intently at the incident and the condition of the affected families he saw more clearly till he saw the 'big picture' in the seemingly small thing.

He saw that if he could only loan out $27 the fate of these 42 families would change for good. And he did that. Then he did some more for some more families. Again, after sometime he did it for some other families. Soon it became a movement that culminated into the concept of the Grameen Bank that significantly changed the lives of many. By this he solved a nagging problem of abject poverty, made history and earned the Nobel Prize.

To me this is what "seeing the big picture" or seeing the unfolding future is all about though we cannot exactly predict how the future would unfold. Seeing something small very closely with clear intention, intently feeling it and thinking of the 'big picture' of how to make sense of it paves the way for the future to unfold from the 'long now' since the future is enfolded in the 'long now'.

Helping a better future to unfold depends on seeing the 'big picture' in seemingly small things that are right before our own eyes. And from that 'big picture' of 'small things' other relevant details emerge spontaneously to breathe life into an emerging future.

Is there a lesson to be learned from the way Md. Yunus saw the issue?

Chapter 5

Patterns to No-Patterns

"Seeing gaps between patterns is as important as seeing patterns. Patterns & no-patterns."— @predictswan

As humans we are so adept at noticing patterns; forcing us to act upon them or upon the information they provide; informed by our emotional and cognitive memory of similar events. And we have really come to believe that our thinking must always be based on recognizing patterns. It is not a bad idea, anyway. It helps us simplify many things in life. And it has an important place in human activity. It is useful and difficult to do without it.

But what might have happened if Md Yunus relied on older patterns? It is sure that he must have seen similar events right from his childhood since Bangladesh is regularly ravaged by such cyclones, storms and flooding. He might have sympathized with the victims and thought about better disaster management or a better relief system or better warning system. There is no doubt that all those would surely be needed to help people in distress. Those are inbuilt patterns we have collectively developed over the years seeing such events. But that does not help us gain new knowledge to creatively come up with a solution to an issue.

Is that the right way? Fair to say that we are at times, deluded by patterns?

I think our natural ability to spot patterns have consistently deluded us since whenever we see something we immediately notice the outlines of an object that goes onto form patterns. Artists regularly use this trick as one of many to produce their work. We hardly, if ever, notice anything in between or anything connected to the object of our attention. In other words, when we see outlines of something, we do indeed notice the patterns being formed by the outlines but fail to see the sound of tree falling in the background.

If this informs our judgment, decision making or creative designs we are bound to go wrong.

Let us see what Bateson says about this phenomenon.

He explains the role of unconscious tremors, which he calls 'saccades' of our eye balls.

He says, "The end organs are thus in continual receipt of events that correspond to 'outlines' in the visible world. We draw distinction, that is, we pull them out. Those distinctions that remain undrawn are not noticed or seen. They are lost forever with the sound of the falling tree . . . ."

Today, the world around us moves so fast that there is hardly any pattern that stays long enough with us to inform our judgments, decisions, thinking and creative efforts.

So this is a peculiar situation we are faced with—To see or not to see Patterns? Or how do we see and act on No-Patterns?

A Pattern initiates our 'thinking' (stored images) that informs our actions.

A 'No-pattern' turns on our 'feelings', which then turns on our imagination leading us to come up with something creative; appropriate for the situation we are 'seeing.'

It would be interesting to see whether 'feelings' or 'thinking' would take the center-stage of our human activities from now on.

I feel it would be 'feelings' first followed by 'thinking' not the other way around. It only helps us to remain human and not behave like a robot armed with technology and predetermined responses.

So, in 'seeing', both patterns and 'no-patterns' assume great importance. To get stuck with either might prove to be a big mistake when taking action.

Study of Patterns

Study of Patterns is central to whatever we think and do.

The interdependent state of Nature is reflected through the various patterns she continually creates as per context.

Leonardo da Vinci was a keen student of Nature. Instead of trying to dominate nature, as we have been trying for ages, Leonardo's intent was to learn from her as much as possible. He was struck by the beauty he saw in the complexity of natural forms, patterns, and processes. He was intently aware that nature's ingenuity was far superior to human design.

And this is what he had to declare about her:

> "Though human ingenuity in various inventions uses different instruments for the same end, it will never discover an invention more beautiful, easier, or more economical than nature's, because in her inventions nothing is wanting and nothing is superfluous."

This inspires me to observe systems at work, think deeply and design and execute effectively.

However, the idea of understanding and learning starts with discovering the underlying principles at work. In order to do so, we must find the invisible relationships between different elements. Seeing through relationships creates the necessary 'wholistic' understanding for us to become wiser and probably enlightened thinkers, designers, executives, salesmen, leaders and workers.

How do we do that? Nature or any form, which is a part of nature, is beautiful because she expresses herself in myriad patterns. It is through the study of patterns that we come to discover the innumerable relationships that exist between different elements. This is perhaps the first and the most crucial step towards understanding and learning anything.

Fortunately, Nature expresses herself in three simple forms. She dances or flows (oscillates). She shares energy (dissipation). She dies (wear and tear process).

She expresses herself when any system is either in dynamic equilibrium or when a system is taken away from equilibrium—the only two possible living states for any system.

It does not matter whether we observe such patterns in engineering or elsewhere. It is still Nature at her best, exhibiting her wildest, creative expressions.

Let us take an example. Suppose we want to 'see' a city. There are many ways of seeing a city. We can see the patterns of deterioration of a city (wear and tear and dissipation). We can see how spaces emerge (oscillation). We can see the movement of people across a city (oscillations). We can also see the flow of money (dissipation and oscillation). And we can see how traffic and mobile connections flow (oscillations).

Let us assume for a moment that our intention is to see generation of heat within a city. For that, we may use infra-red thermal imagers to extend our sense of seeing. With such imagers we are able to take 'heat pictures' at different locations of the city at different times of the day to find patterns as well as no-patterns.

For a person interested in climate change perhaps the total heat radiated by a city in the environment might be enough data for him to see. But let us imagine ourselves to be urban planner and architects. Then we would take care to pour through the images to see a number of things. We may be interested to see areas that radiate maximum or minimum amount of heat. Out of many things that we might care to notice we might be specifically interested to see 'heat islands', where the heat gets locked up and gradually builds up over time. We know that unusual heat buildup might cause significant changes in weather patterns that can cascade into disasters. For example, unusual heat buildup over Moscow a few years back, caused heavy rains, mudslides and landslides in Pakistan, Northern India and China that disrupted the lives of many.

Okay. We get the idea.

Now, many questions might arise, some of which might be the following:

a) How to dissipate the heat from the 'heat islands' quickly and effectively?
b) What we might do to create better heat flow across the city?
c) How might we avoid turbulent air flow?
d) What is the natural tendency of the system?
e) How do we improve the lives of people by using minimum possible energy?

By 'engaging' with such questions we can then mull over the choices we have within the given constraints to 'exchange' new solutions or new re-designs to improve human lives without disturbing Nature too much. In this way the whole NEME sequence is automatically triggered. However, it all starts with the way in which we want to see reality and the various layers in which it exists. Our intentions would create the difference in the outcome.

Zen koan: What separates the two knocks?

Chapter 6

The perils of objectivity

"Reality of anything is made up of diverse views. Wisdom is about living w/ all views but choosing one according to one's own limitations" by @predictswan

One of the significant ways in which we got around the world was to look at the world in a very objective manner. We did this through the use of language, greatly aided by science.

We used language in two distinct but interrelated ways:—a) used metaphors b) named things and combined words to form a rich scale of meanings.

Hence we started labeling everything we saw and defined them and then compared and contrasted them to each other. By doing so we treated everything as independent objects stripping them off from the context to which they belong and as a result lost the real meaning that lies in the relational context of different objects.

Once we started treating everything as objects we were naturally inclined to assign independent attributes to them. So we feel that a position in an organization must be filled by a person having some specific attributes. Similarly, friends must have some specific attributes to qualify as friends. Spouses must be this or that. Children must grow up in a certain way. Schools must educate everyone on this and that. And so on. There is hardly any room, if at all, left for diversity. Consequently, there is little or no scope left for tolerance to varied human experience born out of diverse views. Subsequently, we start losing trust in human beings and Nature. No respect for anything, which is not 'mine'. We have moved towards uniformity and standardization and in the process commodified most of what was human thus denuding our humanity.

We perhaps overdid this just too much to the level of inhumanness in our relentless effort to banish diversity. By assigning attributes we equated human beings to a stone or a piece of gold. Somewhere in the process we forgot that human beings 'breathe'. Human beings think and create. Human beings love. Human beings change . . . . just as any other thing in the world. And diversity remains to be 'seen', sensed and acted upon to bring out the best of human experience.

What might happen when we choose to ignore diversity?

a) See an original idea and start comparing the idea with something else in an effort to forcefully draw similarity, even if it is not remotely connected. Then we either reject the idea or force the original idea to adapt to the 'previous' one.

b) Think that our spouses must be this or that or children must do this or that.

c) Quote this fellow or that fellow and fear to voice our own understanding; afraid that it might sound incredible or inauthentic or others might not deem it fit to be 'retweeted'.

d) Measure the seriousness of a disease or healthcare by the size of the medical bills.

e) Measure the worth of a human being by the money the person has or the superficial beauty features a person might possess.

f) Say that 'you ought to have done that' or 'you must behave like that' or 'these are the 10 ways to reach the top (without knowing where or what that top is) . . .

g) Think of some Jolie while making love to their wives.

And it goes on . . .

I don't hate anything anymore as much as I don't hate a piece of gold or hate a river flowing by. I am amazed how over centuries we lost 'seeing' our own thoughts and feelings, restricting the expansion of our consciousness. Can we bring it back?

The following dialogue between Jon and his mother in "Jonathan Seagull" book acts as a timely reminder to 'see' and know things free from the load of social expectations of conformity to discover what we might be capable of doing with enjoyment.

"Why, Jon, why?" his mother asked. "Why is it so hard to be like the rest of the flock, Jon? Why can't you leave low flying to the pelicans, the albatross? Why don't you eat? Jon, you're bone and feathers!"

"I don't mind being bone and feathers, Mum. I just want to know what I can do in the air and what I can't, that's all. I just want to know."

As we release our fears and need for conformity born out of our perception of social risks, we would start to notice and see things in diverse ways and come up with creative expressions in whatever life we are engaged in.

Dawn Dorinda had this personal experience to share:

"I have personal experience: two sisters move to a foreign land at a young age. One sister becomes fearful of the 'newness' of her surroundings and retreats to the expat community, where she finds familiarity and thus security. The other sister curiously sought out the local community, learning the language and culture and thus grew exponentially in the new experience.

Fear closed the eyes and heart of one and curiosity opened the eyes and heart of the other. How can we teach our next generation to open their eyes to the beauty of individuality and thus open their hearts to more collaborative world, where shared knowledge is true power? The perennial paradox of self awareness requiring self awareness continues to trap many in a tail chasing existence."

Some things to ponder:—

1. What threatens sensitivity of exchange between human beings? Is it the use of depthless,

commodified, instantly legible words of the market or lack of trust?

2. Apart from environmental issues, diseases, political & social oppression what are the perils that threaten our extinction? Would those be 'too much emphasis to see things in one way'; intolerance to human 'experience' & 'diversity'?

3. Is it that in our present world of fleeting perceptions & instantly consumable events nothing stays long enough to form the much needed rich human experience?

4. Has modernity stripped us of myth, magic, kinship, tradition, solidarity to denude the human in us completely?

5. Do memory and imagination offer slippery paths in seeing anything in the right perspective?

A Zen story:

A king invited Zen Monk Ikkyu to a banquet. Ikkyu arrived dressed in his beggar's robes. The host, not recognizing him, chased him away. Ikkyu went home, changed into his ceremonial robe of purple brocade, and returned. With great respect, he was received into the banquet room. And then when the king asked him to take a seat, he put his robe on the cushion, saying, "I expect you invited the robe since you showed me away a little while ago," and left.

Chapter 7

3 Dimensional View & our 11 senses

"Once there is self-awareness, traders can practise improving strengths and reducing weaknesses." by @toughloveforx

A koan: Seeing a flag fluttering, one monk said to the other, "Wind is moving." The other replied, "Your mind is moving."

Here is a news clip from a local daily.

Human brains use 3-D to communicate emotions.

Scientists, for the first time, have identified three dimensions that the human brain uses to communicate emotions. According to a new study, the human report of emotions relies on three distinct systems: one that directs attention to affective states ("I feel"), a second that categorizes these states into words ("good", "bad", etc) and a third that relates the intensity of affective responses ("bad", "awful").

The Times of India, Kolkata, Friday, March 29, 2013.

So how do we put the three parts into practice?

1. We easily notice something that is affected. It might be a disease, failure or a problem or some new development or some kind of movement. Something that is not 'normal' usually catches our attention.

2. Then we try to assess the situation as to how good or bad it is. We do so by noticing the frequency of occurrence. If it happens quite often then we say 'good' or 'bad' related to our perception of an event.

3. Lastly, we try to assess the intensity of each frequency we notice. Intensity depends on the amount. When say "350 people died in a stampede" the intensity of the event in the mind of most people is much higher than when one hears, "one person died in a road accident".

When we listen to a piece of music we do the same. We first turn our attention to the music. Then we notice the frequencies of different instruments playing. Then we notice the intensity of each frequency we hear. When all three are put together we get the sense of the whole.

The same process is applied when we examine organizations. We notice the affected states. Then we notice the frequency of each of the affected states. Lastly we notice the intensity of each frequency. As we club all our observations together we get to see and sense the whole.

This is one of the many ways we are able to see the whole without worrying too much about what the whole really means. What we see in this manner reflects the whole organization; something like a hologram.

Another powerful way to sense reality through our senses and transcend those is known as the way of awareness or better known as mindfulness. This is done by holding down our 'mental-emotional vibrations' to the minimum possible level by freeing our mind from existing thoughts and emotions. In such a state we are neither too excited about anything nor distracted by too many things other than our object of attention. Here too we follow a similar process.

1. In such a mental state we pay attention to small changes and movements. We not only focus our attention to pain areas of but also to other things as well. It is a kind of gently being in focused and defocused states at the same time. We just allow ourselves to soak in whatever is available without forcing our pre-determined thoughts or locked up emotions or pre-formed intentions to take over our attention from what we are paying attention to.

2. We then allow the mind to piece together what we notice into a whole. The whole should surface effortlessly or spontaneously from the process.

3. We then take care to see whether it is helpful or not so helpful to self and others leaving us to choose appropriate responses to deal with an unhelpful situation, if need be.

This can be summed up as a) paying attention to 'see' b) allowing the whole to emerge spontaneously through awareness c) creating appropriate responses to change reality if need be—becoming effortlessly awake.

Whatever way we take, it would involve honing our senses to see correctly and then transcend those to form meaningful responses. As per Indian yogic philosophy there are 10 senses to which Buddha, the great yogi, added one more. That brings the total to eleven senses—all useful for 'seeing' or noticing reality as closely as possible. These eleven senses are as follows:

1. The sense of sight
2. The sense of hearing
3. The sense of touch
4. The sense of smell
5. The sense of taste
6. The sense of movement
7. The sense of replication or reproduction
8. The sense of elimination of the unnecessary
9. The sense of holding or grasping
10. The sense of expression
11. The sense of feeling

More developed these senses are, better is our ability to 'see' anything in a multi—dimensional manner allowing us to act with wisdom.

But what might happen if we were to 'see' with our first five senses only?

Chapter 8

Making sense from nonsense

> In our present world of fleeting perceptions &
> instantly consumable events nothing stays long
> enuf 2 form much needed rich experience.—
> by @predictswan

When we **see** something—we might say—how beautiful
it is.

When we **hear** something—we might say—how soothing
it is.

When we **smell** something—we might say—how obnoxious
it is.

When we **touch** something—we might say—how irritating
it is.

When we **taste** something—we might say—how delicious
it is.

Our usual five senses quickly prompt us to say things
like, 'beautiful', 'soothing', 'obnoxious', 'irritating'
and 'delicious' thus quickly blocking our ability to
experience more deeply.

Once we restrict our experience to only one of the usual five senses without caring to experience all eleven senses, it immediately creates a moderately big problem:

Problem—We stop looking anything beyond the noun—like: a lady, music, apple, carpet, tea etc. It prevents us from seeing what these objects are doing like **moving/rearranging**, **holding/linking**, **eliminating**, **copying/creating**, **expressing**.

To make proper sense of what we are paying attention to we must focus on what the objects or people are doing or the way they are behaving. So, only by using our first five senses we inadvertently cut out the rest six, which are vital for the whole to spontaneously emerge in our mind rather than forcing our thoughts to make sense of the reality. A simple example would be to see an old lady and think how ugly she looks. As soon as we have thought that it prevents us from seeing anything further. It somehow rudely cuts us out of reality. Another example, for instance, would be to observe the effect of tax burden on people. We can keep on debating for hours whether that is a good thing or a bad thing for ordinary citizens as per our perceptions and still remain undecided. But the other way is to see changes in behavior of the people. Do they migrate to cities? Do they use credit cards often? Do they increase their work hours? Do they buy less? Do they use recycled products more than before? Once we focus on what people and objects are doing or how they are behaving it gives us a better picture of the whole rather than restrict ourselves to our first five sense perceptions.

So, our five senses would only leave us with a partial perspective of things that we want to see and sense. It reminds me of the famous story of the elephant and the 6 blind men who sensed the elephant in different ways. Had each one of them explored a bit further than what they did, all of them might have 'seen' the whole elephant.

What can we do?

As we might have noticed, it was the mind that was always interfering with what we were observing. It was always ready to jump to conclusions and make sense of anything even if we have sensed something with one sense only. So, can we eliminate the '**mind sense**' that was unnecessarily interfering and trying to make sense of everything and clouding our vision and preventing us from seeing any further?

Once the 'mind sense' is eliminated we are left with '**nonsense**'. I call this '**uncolored**' or '**no-mind**' state' of seeing reality.

Left with such 'nonsense' we are then allowed to delve deeper and make in-depth sense of things and phenomena that we encounter in our environment and come closer to the 'truth' of things. It helps us in decision making, creativity, design, thinking, strategy, marketing etc.

Isn't **NONSENSE** a wonderful state of mind to see reality?

We all want to make real sense of everything. Don't we?

Why not try **NONSENSE** for a change?

Chapter 9

Learning, aging and leadership

"Every move a young child makes—intentional or accidental—leads to learning." by @MovingSmartNow

Chinese language is rich in their characterization of words. The words contain pictures or symbols that tell the story behind those words. These two Chinese characters represent learning.

The **first character** means 'Study'.

This is made up of two symbols.

The **first symbol** on the top, means 'to accumulate knowledge' by various means and methods, which we usually do through teachers, schools, gurus, mentors, peers and even through self study.

The **second symbol** which is at the bottom of the first character shows a child in front of a door. That means in order to learn one must be blessed with a child like curiosity and innocence. It is akin to the Zen concept of having a 'beginner's mind' with which every situation is viewed with fresh 'eyes'.

The **second character** symbolizes the need for 'constant practice'. Understandably there is no substitute for hard work and constant practice to hone a skill to perfection.

This character is also made up of two symbols.

The **upper symbol** represents 'flying' showing a bird developing its ability to leave the nest. So it means 'to be on your own' and be a leader. This is signified by one's ability to leave the nest.

The **lower symbol** of the second character represents 'youth'. This is an important feature. With constant learning, rediscovering and reinventing oneself one probably never ages mentally and psychologically—perhaps even slows down biological aging.

When we put all the four symbols of the two characters together then holistically they mean—to learn one has to be like a child accumulating knowledge in bits and pieces, which is then followed up by constant practice with the strength and perseverance of youth in order to come up with something original like 'flying' (signifying effortless ease and competence of some skill gained). Then they become leaders by leaving their nests and making their presence felt in the world through their own ability.

However, the most important thing in the whole issue is to become like a **child**. Christ's teachings also reflect the same when he says, "Verily I say unto you, Except ye be converted, and become as little children, ye shall not enter into the kingdom of heaven."—Matt. 18:3

Constantly learning is indeed the 'kingdom of heaven', which is symbolic in the sense that in heaven none grows old, which is just the same as what the Chinese meant by '**youth**' (inability to grow old while learning).

The **process** of **learning** can therefore be divided into three parts, similar to the Buddhist tradition of learning and gaining wisdom—

a) **Accumulating** from a teacher (accumulation of information, knowledge and the path to self mastery).

b) **Self Study** (to be the child at play with whatever one is interested to master).

c) **Dialogs** with peers and friends and **application** in real life (constant practice, refinement,

47

development of leadership and the ability to
stand on one's own feet).

However, the traditional Indian view of learning is quite
broad in sense and significance, which I would now try
to explain.

Celebrating Knowledge—The Music of the River

Possibly India is the only country that has a public
holiday to celebrate Knowledge, Learning and Creativity.

This is more popularly known as Saraswati Puja (Puja
means offering of anything surplus, which in this case
is of love and deep respect). Saraswati is the Goddess of
Knowledge representing speech and creative expression
of science and arts. Most things in India are symbolic
and the image of Goddess Saraswati is not an exception.
The image is therefore a metaphor or representation of
what knowledge is all about.

Well, as most things in India, the story goes back
thousands of years to the era of the Vedas, which most
historians agree was around 5000 years ago.

A group of wise sages was travelling all night. Just as
the day was about to break they reached a river. The
river was gently and rhythmically making its way down
the snow clad Himalayas. The water was pure and
sparkling. As it gushed over the numerous pebbles, it
encountered in its way, a sweet tinkling noise emanated.
They could see the bottom of the river clearly and were

fascinated by the numerous ripples that danced around merrily, occasionally catching the glitter of the sun rays as the sun peeped over the distant hills.

They were mesmerized by the whole experience. It suddenly struck them that knowledge had the exact characteristics of what they just experienced. How was that?

They realized that knowledge is dynamic and always changing and flowing like the river. One can't capture it. It can't be imprisoned. If held, it soon loses its freshness and flow.

They understood that knowledge is a product of numerous ongoing interactions that produced music. Power of knowledge comes from the interactions. The music is only produced by the flow going against the resistance offered by the pebbles. More the obstacles/interactions (pebbles) more subtle and more varied are the musical tones. The deep experience provided them the insight that knowledge develops through repeated movements of passing over the numerous interactions only to emerge through this chaotic process in the form of waves.

It was also clear to them that the primary source of knowledge was through clear observation, involving all our senses—an understanding gleaned from the transparent flowing waters. Everything was observable but transient and ever changing.

They likened the occasional glitter of the sunrays ricocheting off the waves to the sudden flashes of insights that create new knowledge.

Such a splendid metaphor remained with them for years before they decided to give some physical form to it so that people recognize the importance of knowledge in their lives and live with a vision or mental image to go for it and develop it themselves. With this in mind, they came up with the splendid image of the Saraswati.

The image of the beautiful lady represents the creative nature of knowledge, the force behind all human activities.

The swan reminds us of the river and also the sharp discriminating power needed to gain insight and knowledge. This is because a swan has a strange ability. If offered a drink of milk with water a swan would drink the milk without taking in a drop of water. It can separate the two. In other words, knowledge helps us to discriminate between the real and the unreal.

The musical instrument, called the veena (a much older form of the present day sitar), reminds us of the music of knowledge as it flows over pebbles and obstacles. It also denotes the mind-body-spirit complex through which any learning is played out and experienced to gain knowledge. This is a great understanding.

The symbol of the white lotus is significant. While the whiteness of the lotus stands for stainless purity of experience in knowledge the lotus informs us that knowledge is rooted to reality which might be full of dirt, muck and darkness from which the purity emerges. It depicts the journey called knowledge from the unconscious or unseen or unknown to the expanding consciousness of reality or the known. No wonder, Buddha after he was asked to describe the experience of his Nirvana, only pointed to the lotus without saying a word.

It is also interesting to note that the image tells us how knowledge is created. This is shown by the four hands of Saraswati. Her two hands are engaged in playing the vina (Playing and Hearing). It means that the fundamental way of developing the experience of knowledge is through seeing and connecting various observations (playing); hearing and doing work that flows through human experience. The image of the rosary that she holds in one of her hands depicts the need for deep mental reflection and repeated practice to gain real knowledge. The fourth hand shows a slim volume of documents signifying that only a small part of the knowledge (the explicit form) can really be recorded in form of principles or sutras (as termed in India), which can then be passed down to others to gain implicit knowledge through the experience of repeated practice.

The scattering and reflection of the golden sunrays on the waves representing intuitive insights are shown in the form of the golden crown that adorns her head meaning that all intuitive insights come from the universal mind. And the halo behind her head represents the energy and brightness that emanates from ever increasing wisdom and expanding consciousness.

So, to summarize:

1. Knowledge is rooted to reality. It then moves from the physical reality through our senses to the energy field of playing, listening and engaging in our chosen domain from where it moves to the mental plane which then makes its way to the planes of action based on wisdom and enlightenment.

2. Like the flowing river, knowledge can't be captured as it is not an object but play of subtle waves within a field since it an on-going phenomenon of the numerous interactions, always changing course and fleeting in nature. Such movement of knowledge is only possible through facing resistance and overcoming obstacles encountered in daily life, generating the necessary music.

3. A very small part of knowledge can be really documented. That represents the explicit part of knowledge.

4. Major part of knowledge is implicit in nature that is created personally by constantly playing in a chosen domain, improvisations, repeated practice, deep reflections, interactions, dialogs, application and sudden insights. It forms the rich diverse field of human experience or the collective intelligence waiting to be tapped into for further development and expansion of individual experience and consciousness. However, it is clear at this stage that gaining implicit knowledge can only happen in one-on-one exchange between human beings.

5. True knowledge in any field can be obtained through discrimination between the real and the unreal, between the meaningful and the worthless.

6. Knowledge leads to expansion of consciousness, which in turn leads to experience of enlightenment and is the creative force behind all that we do.

7. And above all, knowledge must be shared to maintain its flow that benefits all. This is the only thing in the world, other than love, that keeps growing and developing in strength and character when shared. The experience of it is unending and beautiful but can't be precisely defined or described. The more we try the more incomplete it seems to be.

8. Saraswati, the symbol of learning, is a combination of two Sanskrit words—Sara (the essence or vibration) of our own self (swa). It means one who can 'see' the subtlest vibrations within one's own mind and body is tuned to gain the highest knowledge. In other words he is prepared to see the world around him and make sense of it in the subtlest form. So, seeing is always connected to motion and essence. Perhaps now we can understand Mr. Giri's excitement of learning the first note of the musical score of any learning and improvement journey, which incidentally starts with Sa (swa) or the self. Interestingly, both vibrations and essence are invisible to the naked eye.

Finally, Saraswati puja is held in spring signifying the blooming of the hidden, the latent and the unknown into conscious reality just like the first baby leaves that spring to life after winter. Isn't that what we understand by knowledge and learning?

It is therefore not surprising for Indians to believe River Saraswati to be an underground river hidden from view only to meet the great rivers Ganga and Yamuna at Kumbh. Another great symbolic abstraction underlying the fact that Knowledge plays between our thoughts and emotions to elevate us to our true human potential. Those who wisely use it rise to meet their potential. Those who don't are unfortunate.

Hence 'seeing' and paying attention to our own thoughts and emotions, which are the subtlest of the subtle movements, is the very first step in the whole process of noticing, engaging, mulling and exchanging (NEME).

Chapter 10

Seeing the 'serendipity' way

The pond is touched on every side by ripples—from the koi carp's kiss by @daviddayson

With a beginner's mind coupled to our ability to 'see' things in the right perspective comes sense making. With sense making we start going beyond our senses to expand our consciousness. This is where serendipity comes in handy.

While most of us tend to believe that serendipity is all about lucky breaks and luck smiling on us it is something deeper and useful than that.

It is our ability to combine many seemingly unconnected observations into a meaningful whole rather than analyzing the first thing we chance to see or trying to build or apply a preformed mental construct or model to make sense of the present. Serendipity greatly helps us avoid wrong or incomplete understanding of a situation.

The lovely story about how the word serendipity came about is simply remarkable and I hope it would help understand serendipity better.

Horace Walpole, in 1754, retold an exciting old Arab tale as found in Arabian Nights or in the oral traditions of India.

Giaffer was a powerful king of Serendippo, which is modern day Sri Lanka. He had three fine sons. When they came of age he decided to train them by sending them on a long voyage to gain great practical experience before they can become wise kings like him.

One day, they were in for some bad luck when they chanced upon a camel driver. The camel driver had lost a camel and on seeing them, asked as to whether they had seen any lost camel. The princes said that though they haven't seen the camel they would be able to describe it.

They said, "It was blind in the right eye. It had a tooth missing. It was lame. It was carrying butter on one side and honey on the other. And it was carrying a pregnant lady."

Their description of the lost camel was so accurate that the camel driver had no doubt in his mind that his camel was stolen by these three princes. So without much ado he presented them before Emperor Behram seeking punishment for stealing.

In the court the princes explained how they 'saw' that the lost camel was blind in the right eye. This was because they saw the grass was only cropped on the left side of the road though the grass on the left side was less green than the grass on the right side.

They 'saw' the missing tooth from the scattered bits of chewed grass on the road. From the patterns of their footprints they 'saw' that the camel was lame. And since they saw ants lined up on one side of the road while they saw bees busy on the other side of the road, they inferred that the camel was carrying butter on the ants' side and honey on the bees' side.

And how did they 'see' the pregnant woman? The princes noticed a place where the camel had knelt down and they 'saw' handprints on the sand with traces of wetness in between. The handprints and the wetness told them two things. First, the handprints were that of a woman. Second the woman had to use her hands to lift herself up after having relieved herself, which suggested a pregnant woman to them.

After Emperor Behram heard the three princes it became instantly clear to him that the princes were absolutely innocent. He appreciated the way the princes intelligently pieced together diverse and apparently casual observations to create the right image of the lost camel. He was so impressed by their observation skills that he not only released them immediately but also handsomely rewarded them and asked them to stay back as his advisors.

This combinatorial skill of seeing—the ability to combine events or seemingly unrelated observations in meaningful ways—differentiates serendipity from luck. In serendipity, seeing is done in the 'mind's eye'.

So, serendipity is about gaining deep insights or making sense of diverse things we notice or 'see'. With such insights we would not only be able to make sense of the now but also find out what is lacking, which then helps us see the future potential in a far more constructive manner.

Our present and our future depend so much on our ability to develop this skill of serendipity—a vital skill for the 21st century useful to anyone in seeing reality and its various possibilities.

Chapter 11

PLS3D way of seeing through moving awareness

"Reality exists in various planes. Depends on us as to how we move our awareness thru such planes to have total 'situation awareness'". by @predictswan

Of late, the word '**awareness**', made popular by 'mindful meditation', ranks high in public consciousness and is now applied in various fields starting from improving mental and physical health to creativity.

What does it mean?

In plain language it means 'paying attention' to something or 'noticing something with deep concentration' or being 'mindful about the flow' of something and then extending that awareness to different dimensions through understanding, reflection and action. Awareness is not something which is fixed but fluid and flowing.

All that might seem very confusing to begin with.

Actually we move through different states of Awareness. And this 'flow' is achieved in a particular way.

So let us begin by asking, "What are the different states of awareness and how does it move?

The First State of Awareness

1. **Awareness of the Physical**:

It means anything that we can physically sense through our senses. It is generally an object but it can be something more fluid like smelling something 'burning'. Or for example, it might be a simple building or a gear or people passing on the street or the sounds one hears in a city or simply a part of one's body or pain area in a business . . . .

This is called **point awareness**, i.e. our awareness is focused on a fixed point.

In this state of awareness we are using our usual senses or use the extended version of our senses through some form of instrumentation.

In this way we can fix our attention to many fixed points present in a given context, environment or ecology.

The Second State of Awareness

2. **Awareness of Connections and movements**:

Now the awareness moves in a different direction. It starts looking for connections and movements that link the 'fixed point' to other points and pieces in the ecology. For example, if we are aware that we are tensed and stressed out and aware about our tiredness and not too good digestion we may be able to link these pieces of observation together to form a link to explain our discomfort. Or for instance, if we are looking at 'low order volume' of any organization and the waste they are generating in their value creation process and increased inventory levels we might be able to link the three observations to form a link. Similarly, if we are examining a vibration frequency spectrum and we notice high frequency vibration of a bearing and then notice high amplitude vibrations emanating from the fan blades then there is a clear possibility that we might link the two to form a relationship to explain the phenomenon that we experience.

We can then pay further attention about how a movement in one affects the other. Or in other words we understand 'How a change in one creates a change in the other'. While extending our awareness in this stage we also notice the function the relationship does like—a) holding something, b) releasing/eliminating something, c) producing or reproducing something, d) moving or stopping something, e) expressing or communicating or feeding back information or withholding communication . . .

This is called **line awareness**, i.e. our awareness now moves from independence to interdependence focused on relationships and their changes (interdependence) and their interpenetrating functions.

Like in the earlier case we can create many such 'lines' (relationships and their interdependence through changes) in this fashion.

At this stage we are not using our usual five senses any more. We are entering into what researchers call 'one's own perception'. Technically it is called 'proprioception'. Proprioception does not come from any organ of the body but from the **nervous system**. So we go beyond our primary sense perception and start forming a more holistic picture of what we are trying to be aware of. This stage brings into play both non-cognitive and cognitive skills at the same time. It is a process through which we start extending our minds or consciousness.

The Third State of Awareness

3. **Awareness of Contexts, Perspectives and Feelings**:

From '**line awareness**' we now move to '**surface awareness**'. This happens when we put many 'lines' together. This is quite similar to what we do in geometry. For example when we place three lines together we get a triangle. Similarly by placing four lines together we get a square or a rectangle and so on.

Likewise, when we relate different parts of our 'line awareness' together we form a '**surface awareness**' of the context. At this state of awareness we form a perspective or understanding or a point of view. With each 'surface' we have a different perspective. So with multiple 'surfaces' we create and hold together different 'perspectives' or view points. The idea at this stage is to increase the number of perspectives (**diversity**) so that we reach closer to a fuller and more holistic experience of understanding a phenomenon or context we started out to explore.

Like in earlier cases of point and line awareness, we aim at developing as many surfaces as possible to get multiple views or perspectives on something. We are consciously encouraging **diversity** to view complexity of given reality. This is the stage where we have gone beyond our primary 'senses' and 'proprioception' and entered the domain of **feelings or intuitive understanding**. This is because each perception evokes in us different feelings and emotions and intuitive insights. So the idea is to harvest a diversity of feelings about something.

The Fourth State of Awareness

4.   **Awareness of Shapes**:

From 'surface awareness' we move to what I call a '**3 Dimensional awareness**' of a situation, phenomenon or anything we are paying attention to. Why is it 3 dimensional? This is because when different surfaces come together we get a '**shape**' which is essentially 3 dimensional. That is we have captured the reality (of course depends on how much we are able to capture) into a '**shape**'. Again plain geometry would help understand 'shapes'. For example, when we bring together 4 triangles we form a pyramid. Or for instance, when we stitch together 6 square surfaces we get a cube and so on. Or it can take the shape of a moving spiral of fluids like gases or water.

In any case we create a '**volume**' (an empty space) by bringing different surfaces together. This gives us a holistic understanding of 'reality' to which we are paying attention to. The emptiness of the shape is the source of the creative potential for any change to happen with all the relevant information existing on the sides of the 'shape'.

Now we can pay attention to the 'whole' and find possibilities of initiating creative change or go for redesign of the system or find ways to maintain a system in a better way. It all depends on possible 'emergence' in our consciousness that either unfolds or remains enfolded.

At this state of paying attention we can have creative **insights** both in the form of **intuition** (non-cognitive skill) and **reason** based on our **cognitive** skills. However both intuition and reason must come from what we are paying attention to and not from our memory or pure imagination alone. This is a higher level of emergence of our '**nervous system**'as a whole, which involves both the mind and body.

Why is that?

This is because as we pay attention to the 'whole' shape, our nervous system provides the insight and our mind provides the 'imagination' and the reasoning based on our understanding, which trigger emotions and energy trapped in our bodies inspiring us to act. So the basic elements—'nervous energy', 'mental energy in the form of imagination followed by reason' and 'physical energy' are called into play to understand and explain the dynamic behaviour of the system under observation.

However, the most important element at this stage is the 'imagination' part. We are not imagining the past or the future but the 'gap' existing between those. This imagination is directed by **empathy**. Unless we can empathize at this stage our subsequent thoughts, reasons and actions would not produce the right results (i.e. right for the context).

The Fifth State of Awareness

5. **Awareness of effortless creativity and joy**:

Armed by the right imagination we are now ready for the last state of awareness that is bringing **creativity** into play to re-strategize or reshape the present. By now we know about the existing imperfections that prevent energy from freely flowing across a system and we also know what 'shape' a system is trying to take fulfilling its urgent need to adapt (by dropping the past). We also know the quantity of **information** that needs to be **changed** along with its **speed** to enable the new shape(s) to form. This helps us to be in the flow of things just as they are and just as they 'want to be'. Through our creative actions we can bring about the required changes to experience happiness, joy and equanimity.

How would we know about what actions would bring about joy, happiness and equanimity? If things become better and we stay healthy our creative actions are right enough. If not, we need to improve upon our ability to 'pay attention'.

However, by now, it might also be self-evident that awareness or the very act of paying attention is something like flow. It is not fixed or static. It simply likes to flow from one state to the other as described above. But like all flows, the flow can be impeded or stopped by **artificial constraints** we set up through our mental filters of likes, dislikes, ambition, desires, aspirations, concepts, preformed ideas, uncontrolled imagination and gross memory that lead to generalization. When this happens we lose **agility** in our living and work.

Once we realize this and try to break up or let go of such artificial constraints we not only become **agile** in our engagements but also develop **resilience**, which incidentally is always built into our physical bodies. So our bodies either reflect or absorb the energy which might either keep us healthy or make us sick and diseased. So resilience can lead to both health and sickness/suffering. Sickness indicates the presence of artificial constraints in form of hidden imperfections that we are yet to overcome. Health indicates that we have identified the real constraints that help our natural flow. Such constraints are to be retained and developed. The same goes for healthy and sick organizations.

However it is also clear that 'human being' is the centre of 'strategizing' through creativity. Hence PLS3D method of awareness lays a lot of stress on tuned minds and bodies capable of innovating. Our minds and bodies are both useful but without a strong nervous energy they can both be rendered useless. Incidentally, the nervous energy is also connected to our **immunity system**. Therefore, it has a lot to do in keeping our minds and bodies in perfect order since all the three together as a whole are fully engaged in our awareness, our normal senses, proprioception, feelings, perception, imagination, intuition, empathy, understanding, insights, creativity, reason, thoughts, actions and perhaps wisdom. One can't be sacrificed for the other.

When practiced to a high level of perfection we live in a liberated state—a state where we love what we get and get to do what we love to enrich our lives, i.e. we enjoy being in the flow of things without attachment to any experience.

It is love. It is **kindness** to self and others, which flows from the effortless effort we experience in the fifth and last state of awareness a state between perception and non-perception.

That in short is about awareness or simply 'paying attention'.

Notes:

1. The technique of PLS3D (Point, Line, Surface and 3Dimensional Awareness) is one of the various technique/tools invented by the author. This has been widely applied and taught in many companies in India with great impact.

2. This is used in various types of settings like—Problem solving, Whole System Design, Strategic Design, Systemic thinking, Manufacturing Strategy, Organizational Strategy, Entrepreneurship and a host of other applications including personal improvement and transformation, which to my mind is the most important application for a better future.

Chapter 12

Seeing in Daniel's way

Whenever we do something that either fundamentally changes our ways of looking at things or challenges fundamental assumptions held by the collective intelligence we are faced with instant denial followed by ridicule before people finally accept new ways of thinking and new ideas.

The 2011 Nobel Prize winner in Chemistry, Professor Daniel Shechtman is a case in point.

His way of looking at things invited denial and ridicule before being accepted decades later. It was same with Einstein.

He challenged a fundamental assumption that 'patterns' repeat themselves over and over again. Many still think that we can find patterns in almost anything that would repeat itself over and over again. Not so, he said.

His discovery of quasicrystals, a mosaic like chemical structure was thought to be impossible by researchers.

While he was studying a mix of aluminum and manganese under his microscope he found a pattern similar to Islamic mosaics that never repeat, which appeared contrary to the established laws of nature as understood by science at that point of time.

Initially he faced such strong objections from the scientific community that he was even hounded out of his research group in the US and publicly ridiculed. But he persisted with patience to do more work on what he saw. Such quasicrystals now form special types of steels that are used in variety of applications like razors, needles etc.

Original seers can take heart from his story of facing denial followed by ridicule before their ideas are finally accepted by others—may be decades after the idea first germinates.

How long would an idea take to move from the denial phase to the acceptance phase is anybody's guess. Here patience and perseverance are great virtues that help original seers accept social denial and ridicule to see what they see.

Have you faced denial and ridicule?

If so keep going since 'acceptance' phase is not far off!

Chapter 13

Seeing fish and rice

To a Bengali like me, nothing in the world is more delicious than a plate of fish and rice. We just love it. The variety is simply endless and the different ways this delicacy may be cooked and presented are simply mind boggling. Well, you can never feel the excitement unless you start enjoying this delicacy in Bengal.

But do fishes have any deeper connections with rice than the obvious connection on the dining table?

I did not realize this connection till I was traveling down a state highway on an autumn evening to visit one of my clients in the state of Chattisgarh, which lies in the eastern part of India. The land was undulating but had patches of lush green paddy fields here and there. Elsewhere, though the recent monsoon has left its bright green cover, wasn't fertile enough to grow paddy.

Why was that? Isn't it a waste of land? Why such vast tracts of land don't bear paddy that might have helped some of the farmers to materially grow in that region?

I was curious to find out an answer to this vexing problem of livelihood. So I started looking for some patterns in what I saw. Soon a pattern emerged from what I observed. Quite close to the few paddy fields that I saw there were ponds both big and small.

"So, is there a relationship between the ponds and the paddy fields?" I asked my knowledgeable co-passenger, Shri Vishnoo Dubey, General Manager, Technical Services, Grasim Cement.

He replied excitedly, 'Yes, there is a deep connection between the ponds and the paddy fields. I heard about this from my friend—a well known scientist who studies ecology.'

The mystery deepened. I was dying to know the truth.

He then revealed a fascinating secret of Nature.

During heavy monsoon, which signals the beginning of the paddy season (since paddy needs standing stagnant water to grow), the ponds overflow and the fishes, who are by that time ready and eager to mate, literally jump out of the pond and enter the nearby paddy fields. As soon as the ponds and the nearby paddy fields are connected they mate with fishes from other ponds and spawn eggs in the shallow, calm and relatively undisturbed waters of the paddy fields. Soon thousands of baby fishes are born. They feed on the mosquito larvae and other small pests that also hatch in the stagnant water. The bigger fishes feed on the baby fishes. Mother fishes try to protect their babies from harm.

A great drama is enacted. It is intensely engaging. Some baby fishes survive, some are eaten and many die in the process. This goes on for a few months and then after three to four months few sharp showers follow. This signals the fishes to go back to the ponds. The late Sept/early October showers temporarily connect the paddy fields and the ponds for the fishes to gladly swim back to the comforts of the deeper waters till the next monsoon when this big drama would be repeated. The paddy does not need the stagnant water any more. The water is released and the paddy grows to display its beauty, swaying in natural melody, in the gentle autumn breeze. Soon the paddy is cropped and it is a time for celebration marked by the two great celebrations of India—the Durga Puja and Deepavali."

I sat stunned by shock & awe as he completed the story! I marveled and contemplated about the beauty of natural systems—the beauty of movement, birth, renewal and development not cancerous exponential growth we are so used to in our industrial unsustainable societies.

But what were the **connections/relationships** between this big drama of the fishes and the fertility of the paddy fields? There are many which are as follows:

1. The fish waste and the masses of dead fish actually fertilize the land through 'nitrogen fixing' while the baby fishes grow in relative safety enjoying the cool shade of the growing paddy. This not only rejuvenates the land but also makes it sustainable year after year helping the unhindered supply of the paddy.
2. The presence of fish in the paddy water changes the PH of the water and makes it most suitable for growing paddy (rice). It is a decisive factor that decides the taste and the nutrient value of rice.

3. Fishes eat on the parasites and fungi and help contain those, which would have otherwise spoiled the crop. They also **save** human beings by controlling the population of the deadly mosquitoes by feeding on the larvae.

4. The phenomenon also **controls** the size of the fishes when they go back to the ponds. How is that? Scientists tell us that when males of any species increase their reproductive effort with unfamiliar mates—a phenomenon known as the 'Coolidge effect' takes place. Male fishes habitually try to mate with new females throughout their lives. While doing so they spend less time looking for food and more time pursuing females. This increases the chance of the baby fishes to grow without being attacked by too many predators. Scientists further tell us that males living with unfamiliar females also grow more slowly and to a smaller adult size and tended to die sooner. In contrast, males living with a single partner eat regularly, grow steadily and live longer. Well the promiscuity of fishes helps in a critical way. The ponds can't accommodate too many large fishes since the existing resources can't sustain them for long. The balance between resources and the fish population is automatically maintained by male fishes running after many female fishes to mate—perfect sustainable solution. On a lighter vein, I could now relate as to how 'Helen of Troy', 'Cleopatra', 'Draupadi' and other beauty queens of human history helped to contain and prune human population at regular intervals.

Chapter 14

Seeing like Einstein?

Here are some of the ways Einstein went about seeing and solving tough, complicated problems, presumably far tougher than the problems we see in everyday organizational life.

I have arranged Einstein's quotations to give a feel of the way he saw through tough issues.

1. Be Curious

"I have no special talent. I am only passionately curious."

Note: Da Vinci's first commandment to thinking differently was just the same—'Curiosity'.

2. Approach from different Perspectives and Levels

"One can't solve a problem from the same level it was created."

"Insanity; doing the same thing over and over again and expecting different results."

"It is not that I'm so smart; it's just that I stay with problems longer."

3. Attention Rooted in the NOW

"I never think of the future. It comes soon enough."

"Any man who can drive safely while kissing a pretty girl is simply not giving the kiss the attention it deserves."

4. Create the Future through Imagination: Not through analysis of the Past

"The true sign of intelligence is not knowledge but imagination."

"Imagination is everything. It is the preview of Life's coming attractions. Imagination is more important than knowledge."

5. Learning by Doing & learning from Mistakes

"Information is not knowledge. The only source of knowledge is experience (direct)."

"A person, who never made a mistake, never tried anything new."

6. Aim at Excellence: Not Success

"Strive not to be a success but rather be excellent."

"Learn rules of the game. And then play better than anyone else."

The 'seeing' process of Scientists, Designers and Engineers is exactly the same. When faced with a problem they 'see' through their minds. They start with 'Deep Viewing' and then perform experiments in their minds; playfully improvising to challenge known solutions and then in the end apply 'imagination' and 'intuition' to come up with really new solutions.

If this is so, why then must we make a distinction between Humanities and Science? Make a distinction between Scientists, Designers and Engineers other than based on the type outputs they render? It is meaningless.

Chapter 15

Seeing like Guru Nanak

Guru Nanak was a great spiritual Master and leader of India.

One day, he along with his disciple, Mardana, visited a village. They were greeted with great respect and well taken care of during their stay.

People came to the master to learn his secrets of living successfully even though they knew a lot about it.

Nanak and Mardana were very pleased with the gentle nature and exemplary behavior of the people of that village.

When the master and his disciple left the village, Mardana asked his master, 'What blessings you have for them?'

Nanak said, 'I wish that this village is completely destroyed and ruined so that none can live here anymore.'

Mardana was shocked by what he heard. But he did not question his master. They kept traveling.

Few days later they came to another village. Here their experience was completely different. People were hostile. They hurled abuses at them. Some even threw stones at them. None offered them food or a place to rest. They even refused them water to drink.

The master and the disciple somehow spent the night in that village under a tree and by day break they were on their way out of the village.

While they were leaving the village, Mardana asked the master, 'Master, what curse would you like to cast upon such heartless villagers?'

Nanak softly replied, 'Did you ask me to cast a curse on these villagers? I would not do that at all. In fact, I would bless them so that their village grows more prosperous and the villagers lead a better standard of life and have more food to live on.'

By this time Mardana have had enough of confusion. He simply could not understand his Master's strange ways of 'seeing' and could not figure out why his Master cursed the villagers who were so kind and courteous to them and blessed the villagers who were out to kill them.

But he knew that his master was a very unusual leader of men. So after some time, unable to contain his curiosity any longer, he asked Nanak, 'Master, I don't understand. Why did you bless the people who were so unkind to us and curse the people who were so good and nice to us?'

'It is simple', replied Nanak. 'The villagers who were kind to us were exceptional men and women. I haven't seen such a group of people anywhere so far. So in a way I did curse them by wishing that their village be destroyed forever so that these good people are scattered and are forced to settle in other lands. This would brighten up the lives of others since they can only enlighten them with their way of living. On the other hand, I blessed the notorious villagers to be more prosperous so that such people are never forced to leave their place to live in other villages. For if they do that they would contaminate the minds of others forcing them to follow their evil ways in thought, words and actions. It would then harm the world so much that it would be difficult to restore.'

I call this way the 'inverted way' of seeing with the right perspective.

Chapter 16

Seeing like Shri Ramakrishna

Shri Ramakrishna was a spiritual master who lived his simple life in Dakhinswar, a famous place in North Kolkata by the banks of river Hoogli. Incidentally, my ancestral home is near this place.

One morning, after his meditation and prayer, the Master along with his disciples, came out of their temple and walked towards the river bank.

There the Master chanced to see a scuffle break out. A group of young men ganged up against one poor fellow and was raining blows on his bare back with sticks. Soon angry red welts appeared all over the back of the unfortunate man.

The Master was visibly overcome with grief. Tears rolled down his eyes. And soon his disciples saw similar angry, deep red welts appear on the back of their master. When they looked more closely they were surprised by what they saw.

The pattern of the welts on their master's back was an exact copy of the pattern of the welts on the back of that poor fellow.

This is a very advanced state of seeing things with great empathy. However, such advanced state of seeing things with empathy is not needed in our ordinary lives. Empathetic seeing involves extending our senses beyond our bodies to project it on the object of our attention. In this way, we can really see what an object or thing or a human being is suffering from. In engineering, we extend our senses through instrumentation. In human affairs we can extend our senses through our imagination. On many occasions I have successfully solved many engineering and human problems through this method of 'empathetically seeing' things and the plight of human beings.

Chapter 17

Not one: not two

Sun & its light
Ocean & its waves
Singer & his song
Writer & his story
Artist & his art
Dancer & her dance
Poet & her poem
Engineer & his designs
House & its occupants
Bearing & its lubrication
Gas flow & its duct wall
Motor & its bearings
Bus bar & its joints
Leader & his followers
Organization & its employees
Working & its learning
Production & its demand
Productivity & its inventory
Earnings & its expense
Problems & its constraints
Context & its contents
Management & its effectiveness
Mentor & his mentees
Cow & its meadow
Mother & her child
Husband & his wife
Beautiful lady & her beautiful necklace

Lover & his love
Bird poop & its digested seed

How do we separate one from the other?
Whom do we appreciate?
What do we change or improve to get what?

Not One: Not Two

We all are dependent on each other but also independent of each other. Hence we are never two and never one. That is the paradox in life. There is no guarantee for anything. We may think of a person in a particular way. But he might do something completely unexpected the very next moment. At times he is influenced by others. Sometimes he acts very independently. The person and what he notices can't be separated. The person and what he produced can't be separated.

My 22 year old son asked me the deeper implication of "Not One: Not Two".

We think that we dominate the earth and nature. We don't. One can't be separated from the other.

We think we are the masters of our destiny. We aren't. None of us are independent. We are interdependent. Hence we alone can't determine our destiny.

We think that the world and its markets are unlimited and we can keep on exploiting it. It isn't. It is dependent on so many other things.

We think history is a process of advancement with every problem solvable. It isn't. Advancement depends on whether we are in balance with others and how history is evolving around the world. And all problems are not solvable.

Hence the deeper implication: it is time that we change our thinking about objects, phenomena, human behavior, history, management and almost about anything.

We can take another simple perspective. Together two elements create something that was not there in either of the two elements that created it in the first place.

Hydrogen and Oxygen are gas molecules. But when they combine they produce water. Wetness is an emergent property that is not there in either of the two elements.

Similarly, Sodium and Chlorine are both poisonous for human beings but when they combine it produces salt, which is good for human beings. This is the emergent property of the system.

Husband and wife are neither separate nor can be totally merged into one. When combined another emergent property arises—a family and its value system, which comes neither from the husband nor from the wife alone.

It is same for every case that we encounter.

Therefore NOT ONE: NOT TWO

Chapter 18

Effortless changes

We all want to **change** something or the other all the time.

Many men want to look and feel like 22 year olds when they are almost over the hill and touching 50. So they try hard to change and behave like a youth, sprinkled with a liberal dose of self hypnotism that age is only a number and try hang around with women half their age. It hardly works, if at all.

Similarly, many women would love to hide their ever growing imagined wrinkles and sagging skin to look like a sweet sixteen through application of costliest available cosmetics till men can no longer read between the lines. That does not work either.

We imagine the trauma of cancer and do our best to avoid the disease by supplementing our breakfast with anti-oxidant capsules and make bold public declaration of giving up smoking, drinking and probably sex. The chance of having the disease might in all probability be decided by the flip of an unbiased coin.

We also don't want to remain poor. So we try with great effort to change our thinking and action by copying the richest people on earth with well concealed hopes pinned onto their rag to riches stories only to find at the end that we were left running on an endless conveyor that leads nowhere.

Many are crazy about going up the very oily and slippery corporate ladder. So we gather around us all types of self help books that promise 101 ways to reach the top in less than 5 years. We all know what might happen. The authors of the self help books get richer by the day while we continue to remain where we were or might even slip off the ladder to break a bone or two.

As human beings we are all afraid of death. Some take it to absurd extremes by changing their lifestyle and probably their inner lives in 8 predictable ways like a) give up smoking b) give up drinking c) moderate love making d) moderate exercise e) trim the fat around the waist f) take cholesterol lowering drugs for life g) take aspirin for life h) change the nature of work. Risk assessment studies show the worth of such careful interventions and changes to be +/– 2.5 years than one would have normally lived. It isn't worth the effort and time.

Most of our lives we try to deal with changes the hard way with lot of pomp and fury signifying nothing. The reasons for such changes are a) Fear b) Social pressure c) Pleasure d) Self aggrandizement. Changes in these lines are always fraught with inherent danger of not working out well enough resulting in wasted effort, time, money and a big dent on the self esteem. Moreover, these are all superficial in nature. We think we have changed the inputs but the outputs don't change in any significant ways. It might, at times, deteriorate instead.

That leaves us with very little precious time and energy to go for real changes, some of which are as follows:

Changes that follow our natural **instinct** to do something very well.

Changes that develop the natural tendency of a movement, however latent.

Changes that challenges us to take life changing **initiatives** for others.

Changes that allow us to live more **authentically**.

Changes that allow us to **discover** ourselves through play.

Changes that spring from our intelligent **insights** and responses to ever changing reality and engaging in something more meaningful and humane.

Changes that are based on the lessons learned from the dynamics of **nature**.

Changes that are based on the reflection of **reality**.

Changes that can bring about **quantum** effects.

And changes that may be done almost **silently from within**.

These, fortunately, are all real big changes where a small change in the input with the right intention, right notice, right engagement and right exchange has the potential to bring about dramatic and long lasting changes in output.

Surprisingly, such changes call for the minimum **effort**, minimum **time** and minimum **resources**. Moreover, such types of changes can be brought about in **any** human **activity** that we are passionately engaged in. The other good thing is such changes are **effortless** and easy; devoid of fear, anxiety, pressure to conform and egos, which in turn release endless creative energies enabling us to make the right moves to live life more authentically, just as it was meant to be.

Are we game for **effortless changes**?

Chapter 19

Unenlightened NEMEs

We sometimes misunderstand the play of complex adaptive systems. We can become so obsessed with the solutions we come up with that we forget to take notice of the interactions and interdependence between things and how our proposed solutions might affect the existing web of interactions and interdependence, creating more difficult problems for us to tackle in the future.

For instance, in the late 1800s rangers at Yellowstone National Park saw that the population of elks was dwindling. They reasoned that the elks were not getting enough food to sustain and grow. Hence they came up with a bright solution that the elks must be 'forced fed' by human beings so that their population would substantially increase avoiding a possible 'risk' of extinction.

The solution seemed viable and nothing seemed to be missing. So the rangers of Yellowstone Park brought in the U.S. cavalry to implement their solution to hand-feed the elks. And as expected, the solution worked wonders. The elk population swelled.

But that is not the end of the story. As the elk population swelled the elk started eating aspen trees. But aspen trees were what the beavers were using to build their dams that caught the runoff in the spring, which allowed trout to spawn.

Now with less and less aspen trees there were less and less dams and with less and less dams there were less and less trouts to spawn. So, more elks equaled less trouts.

Why did this happen? It happened since we did not recognize that we were dealing with an 'adaptive system' which by nature, exhibit complex but interdependent behavior.

The seemingly 'good' solution' of 'force feeding' elks led to a series of cascading events that were completely unanticipated.

We most often seek to improve complex adaptive systems, sometimes with disastrous consequences.

It doesn't take a lot of stretching of our mental awareness to map our understanding of the complexity of the elk ecology to that of organizational ecology and global economy. Even with our best intentions in place, there seems to be really no way we can anticipate the ultimate results of 'tinkering' with complex adaptive systems.

The important question that we must ask ourselves is, "What conditions have to be in place to actually solve these kinds of challenging problems? It does not matter whether we are attempting to solve organizational problems, or machinery problems, ecological problems, economic problems or grappling with design problems.

For some strange reason they are all complex adaptive systems exhibiting their strange behavior of 'emergence' that cascade through the system once an action is taken.

Robots Run the Asylum

Winter was mild and cool,
Time for fun & play.
But old Mr. Ram was hard at work.

25 years back on a fine summer day
Mr. Ram opened his factory,
So that it never shuts down.

Within last five seasons
Mr. Ram bought or built 6 more factories around the globe;
So that his businesses never close & monies flow.

Last autumn, when leaves were losing colors;
Mr. Ram turned 72.
He suddenly became young at heart & adventurous.

So, one fine winter morning,
He vowed never to hit the streets to the airport again;
Save, visit his oldest factory once a day.

50 years back,
He was the brightest management student around;
Now he thinks all of management is nothing but junk.

So he decides to muddle the mud on the shop floor;
With his own ideas tinged by 'creativity';
Rejecting all that he passionately knew.

One Sunday evening when the moon shone bright,
He had one of his brightest ideas:

Why not have three Works Managers instead of one?

Next morning when employees trooped in grudgingly,
They saw the notice board in awe;
Henceforth each one would handle at least two bosses.

By afternoon, when the sun shone dimly on the wintry sky;
Managers were crest fallen—not knowing what to do.
Employees smiled clearly knowing the path ahead.

By Friday evening the air was chill,
Productivity went through the floor;
As lunatics ran the asylum.

Darkness fell, stilling everything around,
Motion came to a grinding halt.
Robots moved everywhere not knowing where to go.

Sheila and her creativity

Sheila wanted to live a very creative life. She was almost fanatical and hysterical about it. Why was it? She thought that by becoming creative she could escape the vagaries of life and the associated pain and void she experienced being a wife, a mother and a professional.

Having decided to spend the rest of her life being creative, she was in search of teachers who could give her some headway into the fantastic creative life she imagined to live in all earnestness. She started searching for the best teachers in the field of creativity. The search itself became a serious passion for her. She took creativity to be a 'gift' of some sort available only a select few, who if they accept her as a good disciple might kindly teach and initiate her in their creative domains.

So she carefully thought of creative fields she might like engaging in, like—art, painting, poetry, dancing etc—whatever came to her easily. To her, these were the only creative fields worth engaging. However, she never ever considered her engineering field to be 'creative' enough to qualify herself as a creative person though she was engaged in designing buildings, airports, communities, water systems etc.

To add to her misery, she was never quite sure about the level of 'creativity' or creative attainment of the teachers she went to. After all, she was seeking the very best teachers. She thought that such teachers must have attained a very high order of spirituality to pass down their well kept secrets to her. The idea of 'gradient' for water to flow smoothly stuck firm in her engineering mind.

So, she had a nice plan to test out the 'creativity' of her proposed teachers before she would decide to seriously learn from them. She had a friend who was a 'tarot card' reader and another friend who could 'see' into the future or regress effortlessly into the past and predict both.

After she had found a probable teacher, she would eagerly ask her friends to assess the creative and spiritual attainment of the 'teacher' that would help her decide whether to learn from him. If they said it was OK then she would leave no stones unturned to join the 'creative' class of the chosen person and pay any amount for it without considering whether it was worth that amount or even reasonable enough.

However, she had one big problem. She would learn painting for some time only to leave it after some months. Then, in the very next month she would take up poetry with fervor only to drop it after a fortnight of intense effort before she would jump into taking dancing classes. After a while, she would get totally confused and probably exhausted. It was a tough time for her deciding which creative activity she should adopt in her life.

Sheila was a shade under forty. So dancing sometimes hurt her knees. And she did not have much space in her house for any free flowing dance form. Painting was not only making a heavy demand on her time and concentration but also wasn't drawing enough appreciation from her friends. Writing poetry wasn't a good idea for her after all, she thought. She wrote in her vernacular language, which would not draw the attention of the multilingual crowd of her Facebook's 'friends' to read and appreciate her creative talent. She was in a fix—strangled by a dilemma—unable to decide what exactly to do and how to fulfill her long standing urge and demand for shooting into limelight and fame and be well recognized as a creative nerd.

There was another big problem. Like the way she changed her love for different creative fields she also fell in and out of love with the teachers who 'taught' her being 'creative'. This often led to strained, broken and painful relationships that often made her wake up in the night and cry silently with her face deep in her pillow. It made her all the more restless and uneasy.

Sometimes, while watching the tiny sparrow, prancing from one branch to the next, she would sigh in despair, 'Would I not be able to lead a creative life?'

Here is a classic case that clearly highlights the myths behind 'creativity', which are as follows:

a) **Creativity is a 'gift or a special talent' reserved for only a few.** Hence many, like Sheila, want to be that someone with that special 'gift' or 'talent'. Isn't there a 'war on talent' in the market?

b) Creativity is found and practiced in some specific and recognized fields like—music, singing, dance, art, film, painting, drama, theater, design, inventions and innovations. For other fields it isn't even worth mentioning. Isn't modern management literature awash with the concept that everyone, worth the salt, need to be 'creative' beyond any reasonable measure of doubt? That would help us secure great jobs. By now, most of us are indoctrinated into believing that working in mundane industrial age organizations is just a kill joy where not a shred of creativity exists.

c) **Creators get to the essence of life.** What a wonderful thing that might be! Therefore, being creative is to enjoy the 'true' essence of life, whatever that might mean. Isn't that something to gun for with all vigor and enthusiasm with every ounce of energy we are left with?

d) Creators are a bit crazy. Of course the degree of craziness varies a lot. So the usual thinking goes that there is a sort of underlying excitement about being crazy that would help us unwind from the endless boring routines and regimented life that society mercilessly throws at us.

e) Creators exert a control over their works. They do so through their expressions. That is indeed a great incentive to be firmly in the driver's seat. To be in control gives us the wonderful feeling of 'being in control' and thereby being secure. So, by being creative we would be able to exert control on at least some part of our individual life where others can't interfere much with our unfulfilled desire for unbridled freedom and independence.

f) The goal of creators is to make something new. This is a very deep rooted belief, which is very difficult to uproot. This is because we all want to be recognized and appreciated for creating something new which others haven't yet thought about. That is how most of our incentive systems have been designed and implemented.

These five myths that many of us hold in our minds about creativity are not only false but also downright dangerous if applied in our lives.

This is because we simply forget to apply the word 'creativity' to acts as benign as seeing nature, remembering a dream, interacting with someone, inspiring someone, being inspired by someone, helping our children with their studies and learning, building upon a dialog, encountering and appreciating work of art in mundane things, sometimes feeling the quiet uninterrupted flow of bliss that runs within us, expressing our love for our near and dear ones in new ways and at times find some newness in organizations we work for and in our personal lives. It is rather strange since poets and artists have long recognized that such simple everyday acts are profoundly creative once we are ready and open to life and living through the very act of paying attention.

Fortunately, for us the metaphor of **chaos theory** and **science of complexity** help us get beyond such misconceptions and in the process teach us to see something 'creative' about our lives and the way we could possibly live it in more wholesome and creative ways, fulfilling our innate potential to the maximum possible extent.

Cyclones, Rice & Tigers

Two of the best quality saline tolerant rice varieties, Hamilton and Malta, of the Sunderbans (literal translation: beautiful forest, which is the home of the Royal Bengal tiger is the largest single block of tidal mangrove forest in the world) are now lost forever.

Introduction of high yield paddy (non-local varieties) gradually pushed a number of traditional saline tolerant varieties to extinction as delta dwellers preferred cultivating the big produce variety rather than the types that had endured ages of evolution and adapted to the local conditions.

However, when salinity rose alarmingly with the ingress of saline water after cyclone Aila, the high yielding varieties just did not stand a chance. They failed to adapt to the changed conditions of the soil. As a result, the Sunderbans is now going through serious food scarcity and things will get much worse in the days to come.

As the population rose and the number of mouths to feed in a family went up, people turned to high yielding paddy which doubled the crop quantity. Gradually, the cultivation of traditional paddy stopped and their seeds became rare and some of them became extinct in this highly sensitive ecosystem. All this happened in the last 25 to 30 years. The big and false assumption was that local varieties were of low yield types.

We can see other losses too. The saline resistant varieties not only tasted better but also provided better and stronger straw to thatch roofs of the huts of the local inhabitants. Moreover, such varieties did not need fertilizers and pesticides to survive. Traditional organic variety has ingrained pest-repellent properties. The soil and the sub-soil water also gets better and better over the years with less and less use of fertilizers and protects other species in the environment that are dependent on the soil and water to survive.

It is not therefore surprising that the decisions that we take today to determine the way we live and earn affect others in our rather delicate and uncertain relationships of our fragile ecosystem.

What else got affected? The Royal Bengal Tiger is now **close to extinction**. There are now about 1400 of the majestic animals left. 50 years back there were more than 30,000 of these beautiful animals.

Unchallenged Complex Problem for past 4 years!!

Here is a complex problem. I played with this 'live' problem for quite some time and challenged many to solve this problem—verbally of course. Fair to say, it remains unsolved or unchallenged till date.

Would you love to challenge your brains on this nagging problem? Here it goes for you:

A certain factory producing goods made out of rubber decides to raise its productivity. The rubber products are made in moulds that are placed in hydraulic presses and kept there under specified conditions of temperature, pressure and time for proper curing and formation to take place. The hydraulic operated presses have one cavity to place one mould at a time.

The owner comes up with a simple plan to improve productivity. He decides to increase the number of mould cavities in the hydraulic press allowing him to process multiple products at the same temperature, pressure and time. So, he goes for 'two mould cavity' presses and quickly replaces the old presses by these two mould cavity ones.

He then calculates the possible output if he does that. Let us say that he would get 100 products by changing from single mould cavity press to double mould cavity press. That he thought would improve his productivity by 100%. It was a matter of simple arithmetic.

But he is dismayed when he finds out the actual output. It is less than 50% (acceptable products) of what he expected to get. How is that? He thinks that something must be wrong. So he decides to increase the number of presses accommodating double mould cavities.

What is the result? Again less than 50% (acceptable products) of what he thought he must get.

Infuriated, he goes for '3 mould cavity' presses. He then increases the number of presses to 10. And also increases the number of operators and workmen to run the operation. He backs it up by increasing the number of supervisors to look after the operation. He also increases the number of overhead cranes from one to two.

How did that turn out?

Again less than 50% of what he calculated would be the output.

Baffled, he then thinks to improve the system and institute a system of quality culture. He also thinks of training the workers and the supervisors to do their jobs better and pay close attention to the performance of the machines and moulds and the way rubber is injected into the mould cavities—trying to lessen the time and the apparent wastages in the system.

What happens?

The output refuses to move even a percentage point above 50%.

Can you crack this stubborn, nagging and chronic problem for the factory owner? He would perhaps be indebted. Surely, this was a case of unenlightened noticing and action. What would be the right thing for the owner to do?

Fate of a consulting outfit

A consulting wing of a famous University continued with their fabulous performance year after year. It had a small group of very experienced and knowledgeable faculty members, led by a very innovative Professor. They blazed ahead with their pioneering paradigm. Soon they were recognized the world over as 'thought leaders' in their field. They did a small number of high value consulting jobs, which was sufficient to turn over a handsome profit. However, the business centered on innovative solutions offered to their clients to improve their productivity and lower their costs.

Years rolled by. As business grew, younger consultants filled the ranks. They were competent enough to take the business miles ahead than what it were in the initial days. After some time, the young geeks thought to expand the business globally. They thought that offering training programs would quickly improve their performance and profitability. Moreover, as soon as training programs were standardized they would not need to deliver those through high paid experienced consultants. In that manner they would also be able to contain costs.

In a short time, the training programs were designed, standardized and commodified. Business boomed, just as they thought. It seemed there was no stopping them. Then a strange thing happened. Four years on others started copying their standardized, commodified training modules and started offering those to the clients at a cheaper rate. The phenomenon of copying and cutting price snowballed. The once formidable consulting wing of the University could no longer keep pace with their competitors and compete on a level playing field.

Their business soon folded up. And the once famous consulting wing, which by that time has become autonomous, went into administration and closed down forever.

Chapter 20

Seeing like Gandhi

Mahatma Gandhi serves as a great example of embracing emerging strategies to address social issues, which is the cornerstone of *Nemetics* approach to complex problems. I would like to highlight Gandhian strategy in three critical areas, which are as follows:

a) Gandhi's strategy about **uplifting the poor**.
b) Gandhi's strategy about **children education**.
c) Gandhi's strategy on **Indian Independence**.

It is interesting to note that Gandhi never ever had any fixed ideas or concepts about these social issues. His strategies simply emerged from his keen observation and engagement on these issues as it were during his time.

Bread & Butter for the Poor

First, let us explore Gandhi's strategy for uplifting the poor. He understood that there was little or no point of talking about ethics, morals, religion, spirituality or philosophy to the poor, though he himself was a very spiritual man. He also shunned the idea of placing before them any sort of 'collective vision'. Why so? Because he thought that by doing any of these he would be simply 'cheating' people since reality was completely different.

He saw that more than 80% of Indians were very poor with hardly any good food to eat much less nutritional food. The poor could somehow manage the 'bread' as he said but were unable to have the butter to go along with it. With this came his simple realization that to the poor 'Food is God'.

He then set his mind to come up with means for the poor to get the butter. And that wasn't very easy under British rule. They hardly cared about the poor masses since their only concern was to amass money for Britain. So what could be done? He then hit upon a simple plan. Every villager would have a 'charka' (a simple inexpensive spinning wheel) with which they could spin out yarn which is then sold to the local hand looms for turning the yarn into garments, which could then be sold in the local market. A part of the profit was to be shared with the poor people who provided the yarn spun on their charkas.

The idea caught on and soon became a success much to the chagrin of the British rulers since their money spinning textile industry was threatened. The appeal to people became effective since the villagers had lot of time on their hands. They had very little to do between sowing seeds and harvesting. That idle time was properly utilized within the given constraints to bring 'butter' home.

However, Gandhi didn't relax after exchanging the idea. He and his friends were all engaged in spinning yarn through the 'charka'. Over time, it soon became a symbol to which people could easily relate to and unite.

This was a great feat since uniting so many people enjoying great diversity is no doubt a very difficult task. People were simply proud to spin the wheel. I heard from my father how as a school boy he was so inspired by Gandhi that he was busy with his spinning wheel two hours a day every evening after he was back from school instead of spending his time swimming, which was his favorite sport.

I think this was probably the first networked co-operative movement in the world aimed at economic improvement of the masses. Certainly it wasn't a small feat. This simple but powerful idea soon caught the fancy of a young boy named Verghese Kurien. When he grew up he started the world's first milk co-operative movement which is today the world's largest producer of milk and milk products. In India this is known as the 'white revolution'.

How is the Gandhian strategy of co-operative movement applied to this area? Every morning before sunrise around 3 million village women bring to the Amul factory whatever small amount of milk they could milk from the few cows they have in exchange of good money, which is more than they could have otherwise got by selling their product in the local market. From such small contributions Amul then produces milk and milk products distributed all across India.

Children Education

Now we come to the next strategy that emerged for educating children of India. He noticed that the traditional 'caste system' was a big constraint for the unity of India. Upper caste people simply refused to mix with the lower caste people and the lower caste people were alienated from the main stream. This was not only sad but also would prove to be a disaster if India were to progress, he thought. The lower caste people mainly comprised of various types of artisans, who made up more than 60% of the population. How was he to bring them together?

A strategy emerged through his skill of noticing reality He would aim to do so through children education. How was it? In India, every village is known for its mastery of some craft or the other. That is how they survived for centuries. For example, if one village mastered making earthen pots and utensils then another village was famous for making cotton garments, or polishing gem stones or well known for smithy work. Gandhi wanted these crafts to survive. So he designed his education system around the craft the village was famous for. He insisted that every child of the village would master the craft of the village along with other subjects like Mathematics, Science and Languages. He was clearly aiming at integration at various levels.

At the most basic level, he wanted the higher castes to integrate with the lower castes by at least appreciating the work that made the place well known. He also wanted to integrate modern subjects with the traditional subjects so that cultural continuity remains without creating a scarcity of teachers to teach the children. However, to my mind the greatest integration he aimed for was to integrate 'noticing' and 'doing', 'empathy' and 'reason', traditional and the modern, poor and the rich, west and the east and above all integration of collective innovation and sustainable economy by building on each other's innate strengths without the aim of mass production. It was simply a grand strategy which his disciples failed to appreciate and implement after his death. If India would have adopted this strategy she would have been a glorious example of what a sustainable economy might look like in these days of world wide economic crisis. His clarion call on this issue was, 'Man's needs may be fulfilled but not his greed'. How true these words ring today!

However, I believe that this brilliant strategy can still serve as a blue-print on which sustainable economies and societies can be redesigned and rebuilt to save our planet, save ourselves in many ways and save our future generations too. I think the last evidence of implementation of this brilliant strategy can be seen in fragments in Tagore's Shantineketan, where the old seamlessly merges with the new. That was Tagore's dream. My father was so enamored by that dream that he planned to send me as a child to Shantineketan for my schooling. But my mother would have none of that. She simply refused to let me leave home. However, I partially made up for that by frequenting that place to soak up the richness of such bold and cherished thoughts born out of noticing reality in its most intimate form. I can still feel it stir in me, patiently waiting for an expression at the right time.

Indian Independence

Lastly, we would explore his emerging strategy towards gaining independence of India from the British. It would strike odd that he did not start out with any concept or idea of how to gain freedom from the British like many others did. He did not harbor any idea of collective revolution or armed revolution or mass uprisings.

His first approach was to persuade Britain to grant dominion status to India like it did for Australia and other countries. He peacefully pursued this for several years till it was amply clear that Britain refused to buzz an inch.

Soon the second strategy emerged. He would peacefully protest against any further British plans to make and carry away wealth and money from India. With that strategy in mind he started small collective movements against the British administration for anything collective consciousness thought to be an act of exploitation. The most famous in this series of protest is known as Dandi March (or also known as the Salt March). Soon such collective actions were having the desired effect on the general mass. They have found an effective way to stop the British in their tracks.

Meanwhile as Britain entered WW II Gandhi saw the opportunity to take the collective nonviolent movement several notches higher since Britain would now be needing more money than ever before to sustain the war efforts and it would be sponging India for that. He stepped up his campaign and called it as 'Non-Violent Non-Cooperation Movement'. The strategy was simple and clear to the masses. Don't buy British goods. Boycott them. Don't help the British in any way, however small. Use only goods made by Indians in India. Somehow, anyhow stop the money exchange. I remember my grandmother telling me how she, on hearing Gandhi in one of his several public speeches, switched from fancy British and French clothes to the home spun clothes and how she along with her friends made a bonfire on the streets out of 'foreign clothes and other articles such like scents, powders, soaps, face creams, etc. Was it the same grandmother who got her laundry done in Paris? Incredible is the effect of the voice of an authentic leader who could stir the collective consciousness of the masses through simple but cogent words!

By 1942, Gandhi was pretty clear that with the war upon the British they would have no other option but to leave India when the war comes to its logical end. They would simply run out of money to administer India. I marvel at his systemic way of noticing phenomena happening around him. It is at that time he took it upon himself to proclaim the famous slogan that instantly found a place deep in the hearts of every Indian, 'Quit India'. The challenge was thrown and the British were in no mood to accept it.

These two words galvanized India and Indians against the British so as to make their stay unbearable. No fights. No wars. No revolution. In two years time the British were looking for a face saving solution to quit

India, their crown jewel. 15th August 1947 marked a not so peaceful transition to freedom at midnight when India greeted her new found freedom through non-violence, something that symbolized her for thousands of years.

In this example, we see how strategies to win freedom evolved with time through the power of noticing right things in the right perspective.

Lesson Learned:

a) Strategies are not great plans and visions or explicit missions. They effortlessly emerge out of necessity in a given situation provided we care to notice the emergence.

b) Look at the problem first, think of the solution later. It is never the other way round where a solution keeps waiting to find an application or a problem to be solved.

c) The strength of the collective consciousness is the real strength, not money (though money helps). Collective consciousness can only be changed through meaningful and authentic actions not through gimmicks or magic.

d) The power of notice is coupled to 'creative adaptation' as a rule. Small changes in a system's design bring about great desirable changes in the output. Adaptation is always done against authentic constraints. And there is no need to redesign entire systems.

e) Keep people at the center of everything. Involvement, Participation, Co-operation, Engagement and Exchange are the key words.

f) Sustainable economy (satisfying needs not greed), 'Food is God' and education for children are all interconnected and interdependent as a whole to give any strategy a shape and its life. One is not without the other. All meaningful strategies must have the vital change components linked to each other to work effectively. One feeds on the other. They are interdependent and independent at the same time.

Chapter 21

Seeing like Tagore

The way Tagore saw things can be noticed from this dialogue between Einstein and Tagore. This conversation is considered by some to be one of the most stimulating and intellectually riveting conversations in human history.

EINSTEIN: Do you believe in the Divine as isolated from the world?

TAGORE: Not isolated. The infinite personality of Man comprehends the Universe. There cannot be anything that cannot be subsumed by the human personality, and this proves that the Truth of the Universe is human Truth.

I have taken a scientific fact to explain this—Matter is composed of protons and electrons, with gaps between them; but matter may seem to be solid. Similarly humanity is composed of individuals, yet they have their interconnection of human relationship, which gives living unity to man's world. The entire universe is linked up with us in a similar manner, it is a human universe. I have pursued this thought through art, literature and the religious consciousness of man.

EINSTEIN: There are two different conceptions about the nature of the universe: (1) The world as a unity

dependent on humanity. (2) The world as a reality independent of the human factor.

TAGORE: When our universe is in harmony with Man, the eternal, we know it as Truth, we feel it as beauty.

EINSTEIN: This is the purely human conception of the universe.

TAGORE: There can be no other conception. This world is a human world—the scientific view of it is also that of the scientific man. There is some standard of reason and enjoyment which gives it Truth, the standard of the Eternal Man whose experiences are through our experiences.

EINSTEIN: This is a realization of the human entity.

TAGORE: Yes, one eternal entity. We have to realize it through our emotions and activities. We realized the Supreme Man who has no individual limitations through our limitations. Science is concerned with that which is not confined to individuals; it is the impersonal human world of Truths. Religion realizes these Truths and links them up with our deeper needs; our individual consciousness of Truth gains universal significance. Religion applies values to Truth, and we know this Truth as good through our own harmony with it.

EINSTEIN: Truth, then, or Beauty is not independent of Man?

TAGORE: No.

EINSTEIN: If there would be no human beings any more, the Apollo of Belvedere would no longer be beautiful.

TAGORE: No.

EINSTEIN: I agree with regard to this conception of Beauty, but not with regard to Truth.

TAGORE: Why not? Truth is realized through man.

EINSTEIN: I cannot prove that my conception is right, but that is my religion.

TAGORE: Beauty is in the ideal of perfect harmony which is in the Universal Being; Truth the perfect comprehension of the Universal Mind. We individuals approach it through our own mistakes and blunders, through our accumulated experiences, through our illumined consciousness—how, otherwise, can we know Truth?

EINSTEIN: I cannot prove scientifically that Truth must be conceived as a Truth that is valid independent of humanity; but I believe it firmly. I believe, for instance, that the Pythagorean theorem in geometry states something that is approximately true, independent of the existence of man. Anyway, if there is a reality independent of man, there is also a Truth relative to this reality; and in the same way the negation of the first engenders a negation of the existence of the latter.

TAGORE: Truth, which is one with the Universal Being, must essentially be human, otherwise whatever we individuals realize as true can never be called truth—at least the Truth which is described as scientific and which only can be reached through the process of logic, in other words, by an organ of thoughts which is human. According to Indian Philosophy there is Brahman, the absolute Truth, which cannot be conceived by the isolation of the individual mind or described by words but can only be realized by completely merging the individual in its infinity. But such a Truth cannot belong to Science. The nature of Truth which we are discussing is an appearance—that is to say, what appears to be true to the human mind and therefore is human, and may be called *maya* or illusion.

EINSTEIN: So according to your conception, which may be the Indian conception, it is not the illusion of the individual, but of humanity as a whole.

TAGORE: The species also belongs to a unity, to humanity. Therefore the entire human mind realizes Truth; the Indian or the European mind meet in a common realization.

EINSTEIN: The word species is used in German for all human beings, as a matter of fact, even the apes and the frogs would belong to it.

TAGORE: In science we go through the discipline of eliminating the personal limitations of our individual minds and thus reach that comprehension of Truth which is in the mind of the Universal Man.

EINSTEIN: The problem begins whether Truth is independent of our consciousness.

TAGORE: What we call truth lies in the rational harmony between the subjective and objective aspects of reality, both of which belong to the super-personal man.

EINSTEIN: Even in our everyday life we feel compelled to ascribe a reality independent of man to the objects we use. We do this to connect the experiences of our senses in a reasonable way. For instance, if nobody is in this house, yet that table remains where it is.

TAGORE: Yes, it remains outside the individual mind, but not the universal mind. The table which I perceive is perceptible by the same kind of consciousness which I possess.

EINSTEIN: If nobody would be in the house the table would exist all the same—but this is already illegitimate from your point of view—because we cannot explain what it means that the table is there, independently of us.

Our natural point of view in regard to the existence of truth apart from humanity cannot be explained or proved, but it is a belief which nobody can lack— no primitive beings even. We attribute to Truth a super-human objectivity; it is indispensable for us, this reality which is independent of our existence and our experience and our mind—though we cannot say what it means.

TAGORE: Science has proved that the table as a solid object is an appearance and therefore that which the human mind perceives as a table would not exist if that mind were naught. At the same time it must be admitted that the fact, that the ultimate physical reality is nothing but a multitude of separate revolving centers of electric force, also belongs to the human mind.

In the apprehension of Truth there is an eternal conflict between the universal human mind and the same mind confined in the individual. The perpetual process of reconciliation is being carried on in our science, philosophy, in our ethics. In any case, if there be any Truth absolutely unrelated to humanity then for us it is absolutely non-existing.

It is not difficult to imagine a mind to which the sequence of things happens not in space but only in time like the sequence of notes in music. For such a mind such conception of reality is akin to the musical reality in which Pythagorean geometry can have no meaning. There is the reality of paper, infinitely different from the reality of literature. For the kind of mind possessed by the moth which eats that paper literature is absolutely non-existent, yet for Man's mind literature has a greater value of Truth than the paper itself. In a similar manner if there be some Truth which has no sensuous or rational relation to the human mind, it will ever remain as nothing so long as we remain human beings.

EINSTEIN: Then I am more religious than you are!

TAGORE: My religion is in the reconciliation of the Super-personal Man, the universal human spirit, in my own individual being.

Tagore was a man of literature and arts. His way of seeing can be further illustrated from his book, "Meaning of Art'. There he writes the following:

"So, life is Maya (forms), as moralists love to say, it is and is not. All that we find in it is the rhythm through which it shows itself. Are rocks and minerals any better? Has not science shown us the fact that the ultimate difference between one element and another is only that of rhythm? The fundamental distinction of gold from mercury lies merely in the difference of rhythm in their respective atomic constitution, like in their different constituents but in their different metres of their situation and circumstances. There you find behind the scenes the Artist, the Magician of rhythm, who imparts an appearance of substance to the unsubstantial."

Chapter 22

Attention of a kaleidoscopic mind

In Greek, a 'Kaleidoscope Mind' means an observer of beautiful forms.

What if we have a mind that is agile, flexible, self aware and informed by a diversity of experiences and constantly unlearning and learning?

What if we have a mind that is able to perceive at will any given situation from a multitude of perspectives; selecting from a rich repertoire of lenses and frameworks?

What if we have a mind that is playful with the ability to see patterns and no-patterns, connections and relationships?

What if we have a mind that can simultaneously think the causal and effectual point of view?

What if we have a mind that can rapidly switch from parts to whole and whole to parts again?

What if we have a mind that is robust and resilient at the same time, can solve problems of any kind, squarely face challenges without being overwhelmed and create new opportunities through designs by giving birth to new ideas?

What if we have a mind that can see through facades of falsehood to lucidly touch the reality, understand what must be done and then generate the will to do it?

What if we have a mind that understands the unity of all things, changes constantly and is free from the pains arising from rigid attachment to all ideas, notions, construed imagination, opinions, concepts, theories and beliefs?

No doubt it would be truly wonderful. We would be then a 'liberated human becoming'; free to flow in any frame of time and space and without.

But the question is whether it is possible to achieve such a state?

Think of a Kaleidoscope. The various arrangement of tiny pieces of colored glasses reflect and refract light into various forms and patterns that emerge suddenly from nowhere. As we slightly move or shift a bit, the tiny glass pieces rearrange themselves to generate new rapidly emerging patterns.

Is it then possible to move these tiny pieces of glass in a self organizing manner?

It is possible when the mind is still and clear like a mirror composed of tiny mirrors that allow 'light of reality' to reflect and refract on various self organized arrangements of tiny glasses for new patterns or solutions or answers to emerge on their own? The important thing is not to consciously search for an answer from an object of observation but to consciously allow answers to emerge from the reality exposed by our observations or consciousness to be reflected and mirrored through a self organized mind for new understanding to emerge so that meaningful actions can be taken for better living.

For this to happen the following practices are essential.

1. Practice of concentrating the mind at will.
2. Practice of mindfulness meditation.
3. Practice of inspired living.
4. Practice of self study to reach the heart of understanding of present reality.
5. Practice of peer learning through observations, dialogs and collaborative exchanges.
6. Practice of learning from feedbacks by doing and designing changes that adapt to present reality and beyond.
7. Practice of practical learning from all that happens to & around a person through mindful awareness of NEME an acronym that stands for Notice (observation of present reality through forms and feelings), Engage (see through and perceive reality through various mental constructs) Mull (over new understanding of reality and lessons learned and think through to make intelligent choices for enlightened actions), Exchange (of consciousness through

forms and expressions; maintaining balance without losing the ability to change again).

Such a body of practices surely gives rise to a self organizing and attentive Kaleidoscopic Mind that leads us to true liberation and evolution of the human spirit to face life with courage, conviction and perseverance and to think differently and live life effortlessly.

Chapter 23

Nemetics—an introduction

The Infinitely Dynamic Play

Have you ever wondered that we face challenges, solve problems, unconsciously form images, design something new and create opportunities every moment in our lives without explicitly realizing that we do so? Yes, we use our own internal power, capabilities and resources to achieve such miraculous feats day in and day out.

Why then we don't think of using this normal and probably natural process to better understand the world around us, do our jobs better, face challenges more squarely, solve problems more effectively, design things with simplicity and beauty and also create new opportunities to not only improve the world around us but also improve our personal lives?

A little thought would show us that things like problems, challenges, opportunities are all **"emergences"** that appear in our lives constantly as things continue to change all around us.

The purpose of using Nemes and Nemetics is to come to grips with 'emergences', which I believe is well within the reach of almost everyone on the earth. It helps us better understand events in our lives to take actions that change our future to a more 'desirable' one.

To recap **NEME** is an acronym that stands for:

N = Notice

E = Engage

M = Mull

E = Exchange

And how do we use this in facing emergences that crop up in our lives?

Whenever we see or feel anything be it an object or an event or a phenomenon we use **NEME**. Hence any entity of our observation, mental engagement and action that follows is a NEME.

When we see things in their right context and perspective we develop what we call 'total situation awareness'. This might be termed as a **NEMESPHERE** (**nSphere**). Such nSpheres move **dynamically** through space, time and energy fields inviting us to engage in its **infinitely dynamic play** that is continuously **evolving**.

We know for certain that any context does not exist in utter isolation. It always exists as a relationship to other contexts. Therefore, health of an organization is connected to healthy functioning of other contexts such as strength of its suppliers, morale of its employees, strength of the economy in which it operates. Hence different nSpheres are all connected to each other. As a whole they behave in a certain way. And at the same time they also behave independently as well.

Similarly, the context of performance of an individual depends on its relationship with other contexts. For example, the well being of an individual would not only depend on himself but also on others such as the organization one works for, the type of work one does, his family and his society etc.

Since an nSphere cannot survive independently it must then be connected to at least one more nSphere. The **connections** between two or more nSpheres are achieved by connected **nemeStrings or nStrings**, which might be imagined as strings having certain stiffness and matter.

However, when many nStrings are put together or organically bundled together (since nStrings are also connected to each other) they form **nTubes** which are nothing but a bundle of nStrings from which different characteristics might emerge.

But what we understand about **NEME** and how it is used?

N = Notice

So when we start Notice (N) a context or an nSphere we start paying attention to many issues like:—

a) Its form and its movement in space, time and energy fields.

b) The numerous relationships it has with other nSpheres.

c) The continual play of interdependence that goes on between different interconnected nSpheres. The is experienced in the varying tension of nString(s) at different points of time.

d) The trends, tendencies, new possibilities, new developments (however weak or small) and their effects on growth and development.

This act of paying attention is done through the help of our various senses.

E = Engage

After our 'noticing' is complete we automatically move towards engagement or simply we Engage (E) in the following ways:

a) We feel each of the issues involved to find out how things are in reality. We might also use various theories or constructs or models.

b) We assess the quantities and qualities involved in the interconnections and interdependences through direct or indirect observations, tests, measures, estimates, analysis or through experimentation or doing.

c) We try to determine or trace the evolutionary history of the nSphere(s) moving through space, time and energy fields. Our intent is to find out what were the previous states and how did it evolve to its present state.

d) We also try to determine what might be the future evolution or development stages of the present nSphere since in the future the existing nSphere would evolve to a more complex plane of existence, negating their present forms.

e) What would be the levers or triggers that might help accelerate its potential movement, however small at present, towards a future state of existence either 'desired' or natural.

M = Mull

The next stage is Mull. In this stage we enter into a more complex understanding obtained by placing the nSphere in its own environment of activity (authentic) that would involve the following:

a) Application of our power of discrimination devoid of any emotional coloring of our thoughts.

b) Application of our power of insights obtained through intuition, analysis, synthesis, dialogs etc.

c) Application of our will and intention to do something about creating a preferred desired future by using 'levers' or accelerate or decelerate its movement, maintaining or adapting to the present reality or destroying the present reality to release self organizing capabilities of the nSpheres.

d) Making intelligent choices between possible solutions that might create the most effective changes.

e) Communicating our insights, intentions and vision to others.

E = Exchange

Now we come to the final stage of a NEME, i.e Exchange (E). We also term an exchange as **Nemeexchange (nEx).**

The final stage involves the following:

a) Design additional value that would help us to create the future with the least effort, time and resources.

b) Communicate with relevant stakeholders of the 'context' in order to engage them in the transformation process.

c) Implement the action plan/design in various forms to create value in reality.

d) Exchange the value in terms of money/barter, learning, understanding, helping, sharing, creating further opportunities etc.

e) Check back on the effect of the exchange for the next NEME engagement since the dynamic play of the nSpheres is never quite over.

I have tried to describe the discipline and practice of **Nemetics** very briefly.

We may use or apply the practice of Nemetics in the following ways (not exclusive):

1) **Understand** complex issues to unravel the depths of complexity or discover the essence behind seemingly complex issues.
2) **Solve** problems both simple and 'wicked'.
3) **Innovate** to improve existing conditions.
4) Make present reality more **relevant.**
5) **Design** goods, services, experiences, policies and the like for a 'desirable' future.
6) **Adapt, Maintain** or increase our **resilience**
7) Use for **personal** improvement.
8) Improve **reliability, performance** or **profitability** of a given system.
9) Improve our existing relationships for **robustness**, **productivity, resilience** and **reliability**.
10) **Create** social **value** to meet 'unmet' needs (e.g. jobs, work, entrepreneurship, education, health, women welfare and material well being and comfort).

We may, therefore, use Nemetics in various fields of human endeavor like (not exclusive):

1) Organizational Development & Change
2) Social Engineering and Innovation
3) Engineering Design and Implementation
4) Other fields like architecture, services, experiences, public policy formation & entrepreneurship
5) Education
6) Personal lives
7) Health care

Nemetics as a discipline can be practiced as an individual or collectively by utilizing the internal powers, capabilities and resources that are ubiquitously found in every person around the world for the collective welfare of the human society without suffering from long term damages or consequences initiated by our actions.

Chapter 24

Nemetics, Strings & Transforms

In the previous chapter I introduced the discipline of **Nemetics**.

But what is a **Neme** around which the discipline has developed and is still evolving?

To be fair, a Neme or more appropriately called an **nSphere** is not any physical object like a ball or a computer or an apple.

It may be aptly described as a bundle of relationships an object or an event has within it and the intimate and often intricate relationships such events/phenomenon have with other objects and events; dynamically operating in a shared space at a given time.

That brings us to the first **principle** of Nemetics that helps us **see** the world and nature in different or diverse ways. The idea is not to see anything in one particular way but to see it in as many ways as possible and still be comfortable about the diversity of views and differences they create. It is a celebration of diversity.

The problem of forcing ourselves to see things in one particular way, which is often paralyzing at best, vanishes when we see beyond objects and their simple interactions. Simply stated there is '**no-self**' in anything. So a self is not a self (though it often appears as a form) but only an **entangled bundle of relationships operating at different levels**.

Isn't that true? Each one of us is only an entangled bundle of relationships, feelings, perceptions, understandings and our own mental constructs with which we experientially use at different levels of our existence like physical, mental, emotional, wisdom, etc.

Likewise, every family is an entangled bundle of relationships, perceptions, understanding, family values, common etiquettes, unique behaviors and mental constructs.

Similarly, every organization is an entangled bundle of relationships of policies, rules, human behavior, quality of performance, perceptions, feelings, mental constructs etc.

Though there is a visible form in most cases the **real self** or rather the **non-self** remains invisible, though constantly at work. This is the essence of the reality, the non-self full of relationships, in everything that we see or feel around us.

Within an nSphere are various nemeTubes or nTubes. An nTube contains similar relationships. For instance, Management of any organization takes various actions and frames many policies, rules etc. We can then club all these similar actions of the Management into one tube, which might be named as Management nTube. Similarly, we might have something called Employee nTube or Customer nTube or Supplier nTube etc. Such nTubes exist within appropriate contextual nSpheres.

As different nSpheres are connected by nStrings defining various relationships, similarly different nTubes within an nSphere are also connected to each other by various relationships or nStrings. It might be easier to imagine them as strings of a violin. When taut some meaningful music can be generated. When loose no music would emanate. Such nStrings connect existing nTubes within a nSphere. If the nSphere is an organization then various nStrings would connect nTubes of policies and administration, nTubes of skill and productivity, nTubes of employee performance and hierarchy. If the nSphere is about an individual then the nStrings connect the nTubes of individual perceptions and emotions, nTubes of education and performance, nTubes of ego and love etc.

Similarly, each **relationship** within a possible **nTube** may be represented as a **string** or n**String**, though invisible to the naked eye. There can be a number of such strings clubbed together within an nTube. For instance if my health is considered as an nTube of my nSphere then within that nTube there would be many nStrings like food, exercise, my associations, my reading habit, my dog, my doctor and my environment etc.

Whether I choose to see the nStrings within an nTube or nStrings connecting different nTubes or nStrings connecting different nSpheres would clearly depend on need and the level of granularity and depth we want a context to be seen and examined.

To summarize till this point:

1. There is no self. Whatever exists is Non-self that dynamically changes entangled web of relationships at play. Not to focus on an object but to **see various relationships in diverse ways** is the new world view Nemetics takes.

2. Nothing exists independently. There must be at least one relationship within and without of a non-self for it to become non-self; else there is no existence.

3. These relationships are not only interconnected to each other but also interdependent and therefore continually subjected to changes over time creating contradictions, limitations, constraints and imperfections and elements of 'desirable permanance' in the nSphere of a given context.

4. All relationships are represented as 'strings' that connect and give meaning to create understanding. Such strings vibrate at some rate (frequency) with a given strength (amplitude) in a given context. What changes over time, are frequencies and amplitudes of the various strings, both individually and in various combinations.

Since frequencies and amplitudes change over time with diverse interactions our understanding of the dynamics at this point of time might not be the same the very next moment. How does that happen? It happens because these relationships have energy content in them. Energy content in each relationship might be represented as vibrations of nStrings sustained by continual exchange of energy with accompanied losses and additions through interactions (**entropy** function).

Since relationships vibrate continually (having different characteristics like resonance, damping etc) the nature of the vibration might undergo **changes** over time, both in terms of **frequencies** and **amplitudes** in a given space and context. In other words, though on the whole, vibration in a given space (context) exhibits a pattern at any instant of time the **probability** that the **pattern** would change over time is 1 (one), which means it is certain.

That is true in every case. On a personal level, my **ideas, thinking, perceptions, understanding continually change over time being influenced by various energy exchanges (nEx)** when I am subjected to reality in the form of new experiences, new thoughts, new perceptions, new interactions, new actions, new mental images, etc.

For instance, let us take an organization. Different activities and events (motion) simultaneously go on within an organization under a given space. **Management** is busy framing rules, guidelines, policies, which we can club under Strategic decisions (a bundle of nStrings called Management nTube). These strategic decisions taken by management from time to time affect **human behavior** of the employees, customers, suppliers and other stakeholders (Behavior nTube). And these behaviors give rise to other activities like improvement activities or otherwise that affect **performance, productivity and profitability** of the organization on the whole (Event nTube).

On an organizational level things are changing too. Relationships with various customers change over time. Demands change over time. Suppliers change over time. Relationships with employees change over time. Processes change over time . . . . Such changes clash and interact with each other to produce new outcomes ready to take new forms with the distinct possibility of creating new nSpheres. The same continually happens in Nature.

Every relationship, denoted as an nString, to stay as a relationship must enjoy the 'struggle' between **opposites** a characteristic inherent in every relationship, characterized by its tension or 'tautness'—all of which are continuously in motion to survive. Call it a paradox, contradiction, constraint or imperfection or whatever you will. Without this constant 'struggle' of opposites there can never be any motion of any sort.

Though it appears **paradoxical** it is relatively simple to understand. Think about our walking, a common experience for most. As we walk, different pairs of opposites immediately come into play. The first is 'friction' opposing the muscular energy that we spend in moving forward. If it is absent we would surely fall, like it happened to me on an ice skating rink, the first time I got onto it. Next, is the way our muscles release energy—contraction and dilation of the energy flow. We can see that physically through the stretching and folding of our legs. Then the very act of walking involves 'falling down' and then trying to 'get up'. At an emotional level my idea or concept of 'how I should be walking' or 'how I define good walking' might be in direct conflict with the reality that I sense. That might make me feel uncomfortable. Or I may try to close the gap between the image in my mind and the present reality. In this case too there is a sort of resistance created. It would also happen that at one point of time, with the resistance building up, I may have to stop walking on account of tiredness. And before that happens, I may slow down to rest or speed up to reach a place quickly. The quality of such movements would depend on the balance of energy between two opposing tendencies. So we see that reality exists at different planes. It is up to us to correctly understand and discern these.

Such diverse sets of opposites exist in every single event or phenomenon. Needless to say that understanding relationships and their own internal struggles immediately triggers off cascades of higher cognitive learning enabling formation of new knowledge, which I call **learning** through **moving meditation or moving logic**.

So we may say, every relationship being exposed to the inherent 'struggle' continuously tries to '**balance**' its position somewhere between the opposites but never quite in the middle for any point of time. This act of automatically trying to balance between two opposites and **changing automatically** at the same time, so long a motion is sustained through energy exchange (**Nemex or nEx**), is what we understand as **self integration** or **self-organizing** behavior that initiates all changes.

This in-built feature in every relationship that enables a relationship to maintain balance in motion brings out another two interesting phenomena, which are '**chaos**'and '**complexity**'. How is that?

It is interesting that all such 'struggles' can be physically represented as acts of '**stretching**' and '**folding**', which gives rise to **chaos**. In other words, the surprise possibility known as chaos is present in every relationship we come across. Chaos, apparently a disorder, is triggered by a small change in the relationship in its effort to keep balance and change between two opposing tendencies.

But what happens when many relationships are entangled and play at the same time? It gives rise to **complexity** out of which something that we know as '**emergence**'appears, seemingly out of thin air through interactions. How does that occur?

It is not surprising to find many entangled co-existing, interconnected and interdependent relationships within one phenomenon or event, where each exhibits its own element of chaos. When number of such 'chaos' **possibilities** get together or play out together a new phenomenon appears—something we know as 'emergence'. Such '**emergences**' might take different forms. They may show as failures, surprises, problems, opportunities, threats, value, and even our own creativity, which we exchange for something (nEx).

For example, the economic **downturn** we are experiencing from 2008 is a simple case of 'emergence'. Though we might be led to believe that an 'emergence' might always be a sudden occurrence it might not always be so. The possible appearance of a growing 'emergence' may at most times be spotted through a '**trend**' over time before they finally manifest or emerge. A **leader**'s role would be to spot such growth in a trend and respond appropriately to 'emergence' as an when it appears. Better our response with respect to time, effort, costs and quality, better is our resilience to vagaries of variation of any phenomenon.

Additional principles involved in Nemetics may now be summarized as follows:

5. The whole of reality is nothing but **Space** and **Motion** sustained by exchange of energy.

6. Relationships represented as vibrating strings (nStrings) change over time. That is everything around us is 'becoming' rather than 'being' through release or absorption of energy available within an exchange. Believing something as being fixed is nothing but delusion.

7. In every relationship there is a struggle of opposites where the relationship tries hard to maintain a balance between sets of opposites forcing the relationships to change automatically.

8. Within each event there is always an explicit possibility of experiencing more than one set of opposites at play.

9. The automatic tendency of any relationship to balance between two opposites is known as self organizing and self integration.

10. The act of trying to maintain balance creates the 'stretching' and 'folding' effect.

11. The stretching and folding effect gives rise to the inherent possibility of chaos in every relationship, where even a small change in the relationship triggers big changes. Apparently chaos seems to be an act of disorder but the order is still maintained in a relationship's struggle to keep up a balance between opposing tendencies.

12. When there are many interconnected and interdependent relationships entangled to each other & operating at the same time within a given space, the possibilities of chaos inherent in every interdependent relationship interact with one another to create complexity which is routinely manifested as 'emergence' in different forms.

Before we get any further it might now be important to consider about how we **learn**. After we do that we then briefly touch upon as to how events and phenomenon playing out in a given space might be effectively represented to make our learning easier.

For this we need to consider how we discern and **discriminate** various sounds emanating from various types of musical instruments we hear, while attending a concert? For example, how do we discriminate between the sounds of a violin and that of drums? Obviously, this is done by our brain by a very clever trick. It does a Fourier Transform of all the sounds that enter through our ears (at the point of entry into our ears all sounds are sort of mixed up—meaning all relationships are mixed and entangled together into something not quite distinguishable though it might have a shape of its own).

What the brain does next is to split up the mixed up sound into their distinct frequency components with the corresponding amplitude against each frequency. This process of 'splitting up' a composite signal helps us discriminate and distinguish various characteristic sounds coming from different instruments be it a violin or a drum. What the brain did was to present to us a 2 Dimensional vibration frequency spectrum which is nothing but a plot of frequency 'vs' amplitude that enables us to distinguish different frequencies and discern their corresponding amplitudes.

In fact, the brain presents the direction of the sound too. That gives us the 3 Dimensional effect of listening to live music.

However, the brain does something more. It also stores the vibration frequency spectrum as an image for future retrieval that might be used for various purposes.

Same happens when we see something. The different frequencies of the colors we see are again split up into their various frequency components along with the amplitudes of the vibrations (intensity of the light emanating from the various colors in all their shades). The way it is done is exactly the same as described for sound. And the brain very easily stores the vibration frequency pattern/spectrum for our future use.

The same goes for all the other **senses** too.

So, when we have any new experience the pattern in form of a vibration spectrum is immediately generated and the brain then fetches out the other stored patterns for comparison, discrimination and most importantly connections. Our innate ability to make several connections at the same time by employing as many senses as possible to come up with a meaningful understanding is called '**insight**', which I term as '**feelings**'—an important sense in a way—making sense of the complex reality that engulfs us.

The point I am driving at is: all that we see, sense, store in our minds and bodies are nothing but frequency spectrums in form of **Fourier Transform** (a plot of frequency vs amplitude). Hence all learning that we engage in and store is in the form of Fourier Transforms.

If that be so, why the reality we experience every moment around us can't be represented as **Fourier Transforms**?

Fortunately, this can be done, more so since any relationship may be described as vibrating element, vibrating at a particular frequency and amplitude.

Coming back to our Management example, we effectively have three sets of nTubes (each composed of several nStrings)—all vibrating at different frequencies and each having different energy content in form of amplitudes. For example, we have a Management nTube (A), which has the lowest frequency (activities over time are not that thick and fast as others) among the three NemeTubes. Human behavior nTube (B) as a result of Management nTube would be vibrating at a higher frequency than the Management nTube but not higher than the thousands of activities that are set in motion affecting Productivity and Performance nTube (C).

The relationship, as it turns out, is A < B < C. Therefore it is easy to have a frequency plot of the various nTubes moving in a given space. Obviously the amplitudes reflecting different energy content would differ. But the advantage such a plot might offer is great. It immediately tells us what affects what and by how much (since interdependent under a complex setting); and what we might do to improve the situation. Deeper attention would tell us that A, B and C are all **fractals** of the different events or motions playing out in a given space. That makes it even more interesting. It is also possible to see the effect of combining A, B and C to form a composite waveform.

I hope to continue the discussion in another book.

Chapter 25

Yoga, Complexity and Leadership

Six factors that bring speedy success in Yoga:—Courage, Daring, Perseverance, Discriminative knowledge, Faith, Aloofness from unhelpful company.— @predictswan

Yoga is destroyed by six causes:—Over-eat, Over-work, Over-Tweet, Over-regulate, Over sm & Over-worry.— @predictswan

Yoga is not only what many take it to be—a grotesque compilation of poses, postures, movements, twists and stretches, though these have their rightful place in the practice of yoga.

Yoga is accomplished when we can fluently stop, control, modulate and use the creative urges of our mind and emotions without being regulated and imprisoned by such urges.

It helps us discern or discriminate the essential from the non-essential. This in turn helps us enhance the intensity of our consciousness to see reality as accurately as possible.

What is the use of doing so?

To my mind, yoga helps us enhance our ability to negotiate and respond to **complexity** in very skillful ways.

Complexity is the extant reality which we all have to face. Whether or not we successfully negotiate complexity depends on how well we understand it by correctly gauging reality as far as possible to start meaningful efforts to respond appropriately to a complex situation.

Unfortunately, the creative urges of the **mind** and **emotions** both cloud and help us see and understand reality. Therefore, the goal of yoga is to help us see and understand reality as clearly and as accurately as possible without the harmful interference of our mind and emotions.

Yoga lists five creative urges of the mind and emotions. Each of these have something useful and something unhelpful which depends on the interactions one has with the creative urges of the mind and emotions in a given context.

The **five creative urges of the mind and emotion** are the following:

1. **Gauging external things correctly**. This happens through correct sense perception, by efficient analysis or by using reliable references.

2. **Gauging external things incorrectly.** This occurs through false or incorrect information or mistaking one factor for something else.

3. **Imagining anything**. When one hears of something from someone or reads about it somewhere it is quite natural to form ideas that acquire certain forms in the mind as concepts. When these concepts misrepresent the real thing such misconception is imagination.

4. **When one goes into 'sleep' mode.** Sleep is that creative urge that operates without our awareness.

5. **When one experiences memory.** Memory operates anytime we visualize something which was experienced before. However, as it happens quite often we can misjudge a new experience as a previous experience.

So what might we do to use only the helpful part of the creative urges of the mind and emotions to help us come to grip with **complex reality**?

The answer in yoga is to refrain from having too much interest in mental ideas and emotional feelings. By doing so we may develop the power to stop their 'unhelpful' influences in our actions and applications.

The trick is to persistently cultivate that lack of 'too much interest' and maintain a balance. That is the hallmark of responsible **leaders.**

But that might seem very paradoxical and very difficult to carry out. And it is really neither very easy nor very difficult to accomplish. It can be done through disciplined practice grounded in faith in oneself backed by dogged perseverance.

Chapter 26

Negotiating Complexity—
The Art of Living—
The Nemetics Way

Whether we are running organizations or running our own lives or engaged in marketing goods and services or solving problems it all boils down to the 'art of living'.

Why is it an art?

Because there are no clear paths or clear answers that are obvious as soon as we face them. What we can do effortlessly? What makes us happy? What contributes to our well-being? What makes us go to bed in the night and wake up next morning with peace of mind? Surely, there aren't any obvious, straightforward answers to these vital questions. Every moment we face complexity in all its raw form. Hence the way we choose to negotiate such complexity is an art.

The only way we can practice this art is by close and clear observation of whatever is happening in our lives over a period time. However, we may only do so when we have a) clarity of mind b) realization that whatever we might be doing till now might be all wrong c) and the willingness to practice the art of observation over and over again. When we have had practiced enough we start seeing patterns that have moved us to where we are today.

If we are able to see things clearly we can make good choices and better decisions within authentic constraints. Only such self awareness helps us to take new and better decisions that change our mindset and our behaviors. When we repeatedly challenge and change our mindsets and behaviors in this manner, we stand a chance to change the given reality and thus our destiny. It is as simple as that.

It is also the difference that we see between people, communities and organizations. Some learn and change easily, adapting to new circumstance and situations. Some don't learn at all and refuse to change. Some don't see things clearly and are afraid to change. In between there is a broad spectrum of behavior that range from sheer stupidity to acts of great wisdom. Diverse interrelated and interdependent events, people, emotions and behaviors in our lives create the necessary complexity, which we then need to negotiate with great skill and careful creative adaptation. This takes a lot of internal and external observations to figure out what is going on and what we need to do next. So, complexity is neither good nor bad. It depends on how we decide to go about it.

With this in view, Michael Josefowicz and I created a four-day course on **Negotiating Complexity—the Art of Living and Changing Destinies**. The aim of this course is to show and use the fundamental tool that helps us change our destiny that is most appropriate within given constraints. Many tools are used in this course, the most fundamental of which is Nemetics. Therefore, this course is also called **The Art of Living—the Nemetics Way**. It is interesting to note that it is a 'way' of living and practice rather than a theory.

The outlines of the four days are as follows:

Day 1—observing the Past in the now—How the past creates the present

Day 2—observing the Present—Revealing patterns, non-patterns and fractals

Day 3—observing the Future in the now—Leadership & Strategy

Day 4—what next?—Adaptation and Innovation

Chapter 27

Personal mastery & leadership

The root of the word Master comes from the Sanskrit word 'Maha', which means a person who has put in effort and time to master the mind.

However, to master something does not mean to control something as it might be generally understood. It specifically means winning over oneself.

Hence hermits, sages and gurus in India are known as Maharaja—a man who has won over himself.

I would like to illustrate this by a story of an encounter between Alexander the Great and an Indian hermit, when Alexander came to India.

One day, he chanced upon a hermit sitting by the river bank of the Indus sitting deep in meditation. He was on his way to a meeting with his army generals to discuss war strategies with them. The meeting point was a few miles from where he came across the meditating hermit. After the meeting, which was over in a couple of hours, on his way back Alexander saw the hermit was still sitting there silently in meditation.

Seeing this, Alexander was not only curious but also very vexed. He was curious to know what this man was doing. And he was vexed because he thought how any man can waste his time like this doing nothing.

Unable to overcome his curiosity, Alexander approached the hermit and sort of woke him up by force. The hermit opened his eyes and smiled at Alexander.

Alexander asked him, 'What are you doing? Don't you have anything better to do rather than sit idle for so long and waste time?'

'What might have been a better task than what I am doing?' The hermit replied politely to the great emperor.

Alexander laughed and mockingly retorted, 'You could do something like I am doing.'

'What are you doing Sir?' The hermit asked.

'Well I am conquering lands and increasing my empire and building wealth for my state and my people. After I conquer your country I would be the unchallenged master of the world. What might be better than that?' Replied the great emperor.

On hearing this, the hermit smiled and said, 'In that case, Sir, I am doing something way better than that. I am trying to master myself by winning over my mind, which I would do soon. That I believe is much more difficult and important than winning the world with all its riches.'

Perhaps it is this interaction with the Indian hermit that propelled Alexander the Great on the path of wisdom. It is said that Alexander's last words were: 'Bury my body, do not build any monument and keep my hands outside so that the world knows the person who won the world had nothing in his hands when dying.'

This story contains the cultural seed that made Indians what they are today—tolerant and flexible people who value inner wisdom over outer achievements. That is the reason the great Indian epic Mahabharata represents the tale of greatness of gaining inner wisdom as opposed to outer achievements.

Personal Mastery in anything would mean exactly the same. It starts with gaining wisdom from whatever field of work one might be engaged in. Wisdom and action are related. One can't gain wisdom from thin air. It can only come from realization of the truth inherent in every new experience one encounters in life and work.

Without Personal Mastery no leader is worth the name. One who can't win over himself can't hope to win over others and expect people to follow them.

Chapter 28

Breaking Free

The way we live and engage with the problems in our lives is the product of our thinking. Hence the problems we face on a daily basis are also products of our thinking.

Can we solve the problems we face by the same thinking that produced the problems? Obviously that would be foolhardy. So, what might be done to think differently?

To find out a way of thinking differently we must then understand a little about what 'thinking' is all about and what does it contain.

Thinking, as we know of it now, consists of combining various "images" of our perceptions, ideas, concepts, feelings, symbols and beliefs. Over time, we keep building these images from our own sense of insecurity. More the images more secure we feel. We want to be hedged in by such images and love to call them knowledge, some of which are undeniably very useful knowledge.

To feel more secure, we also want them to be as solid and concrete as possible. Hence we inject into them attributes in the name of objective thinking. So we find out attributes of an object like a piece of stone, gold, building etc. We do the same for people. We call them traits or characteristics. We then live with such images of attributes and use them in our thinking and living in this world. It is therefore, not very surprising to find how such images grow exponentially over a period of time. As the hedge of images surrounding us grows stronger and higher we feel comfortable by the knowledge we have acquired and hold such 'images' to be truths by themselves leaving them unchallenged.

No wonder we soon categorize these 'truthful images' into different dimensions—religious, political, philosophical, national, personal etc. But we don't stop at that. We want to make others secure too. We love to do that by trying to share our images with other in as many ways we possibly can, the most recent of which is through social media. However, all our efforts to transfer images from one mind to another is through language of some sort—written, verbal, images, pictures, movement, etc.

This is where the problem starts. Each mind has its own set of images which the person does not want to destroy at any cost since it gives the much needed security to live in the otherwise harsh world of living. So, each mind, burdened by the weight of its existing images, interprets the images received from others in light of the images one has in mind. Hence while some of the images might have a chance of getting transferred most get stuck or distorted or rejected in the transfer process.

Clearly, the burden of these images dominates and rules our thinking, our interpretation of the world, our relationships and our lives. These individual burdens we wish to carry around also divide us. That squarely is the fundamental part of the problem we face. And what created the problem? You guessed it right—the individual 'images'.

The perception of our lives generated by our own thinking is shaped by the contents of our minds, the numerous nTubes that we carry. That, however false, leads us to believe in our individual existence. This sense of individuality is further strengthened by our acquiring a name and some property, gaining a superficial culture through our immersion in some culture or the other, sticking to traditions and enjoying the comforts of our environment where we live; making us a permanent prisoners of our own minds.

How can such a prisoner be free or exercise freedom of choice? Impossible, unless we shed our so called individuality and be free of the myriad images that we have unwittingly chosen to become the contents of our minds or consciousness. We seldom recognize that the word 'individual' stems from the root word 'indivisible', which meant the indivisible whole. Over time, the meaning got twisted beyond recognition coming to mean a single entity set distinctly apart from the collective. Our freedom does not lie in choosing alternatives from the existing sets of images we have in our minds or combining them in some clever forms. Our freedom lies in freeing ourselves from the content of our minds.

Such freedom provides the uniqueness that is common to all of us, which is simply the ability to be free of all concepts, ideas, notions and perceptions by challenging their appropriateness for ongoing situations on a continuous basis. Having a glimpse of such uniqueness is the first and most important insight that helps us live and face the problems in our lives with dignity, freedom and honor.

Attaining such uniqueness sets us completely free from our self created prison to make us "Leaders" of our own lives.

And the path to find such uniqueness is truly 'pathless'.

But one thing is sure. Unshakable belief in any creed, religion, political opinions, organizations, authorities, institutions, established orders, leaders, dictators, priests, economy, philosophical knowledge or psychological techniques can't set us free.

What is that we are all searching and looking for? We search and look for many things. Surely we look for money. We search for a home. Perhaps, at times, we yearn for fame and recognition. We long for peace. And hope to find happiness and love. But above all we crave for freedom. The Tunisians want it. The Egyptians want it. Libyans want it badly. Americans wrested it. Indians have it. In every case it is a case of breaking free from the past. Breaking free from an inhibiting past is the essence of all 'freedoms' we have ever experienced. Nature is 'free' since she does that all the time. She breaks free from all inhibitions that impede her freedom to act and to move.

We can be free at different levels. We can be free from our childhood. We can free ourselves as adults. We can kick our addictions. We can leave a job or a relationship behind. In every case we are letting go of something or the other. Painful perhaps but we still want it. It is common to all of us. But the most difficult of all is to break free of our thoughts that shape our past and the present in the form of knowledge and experience and bind us like slaves of which we are not even much aware of. Let us explore the difficulty involved and how we might be able to set ourselves free from its constant pain and torture.

We understood that we are imprisoned by our own thoughts, imaginations and emotions. So the only way we might possibly become great leaders is to free ourselves from these prisons created by our own thoughts, imaginations and emotions. The greatest leaders who walked this earth did exactly that. They broke free of their imprisoned minds to come up with new thoughts born out of this new found freedom that changed the way we live today.

First things first: let us conduct a mental experiment to find out how we trap ourselves with our own thoughts.

How the Past locks us in?

Usually when we start thinking we start from 'images' stored in our minds, which are nothing but previous experiences called knowledge. It is useful to remember that every experience is stored in multiple images in different sections of our brain and body in form of frequency spectrums. So, with the help of such images collected from different parts of the brain (a storage device of the mind) and body we try to see a present situation or context by drawing in supposedly relevant images we find in our stores, which more-or-less closely fit the present situation. It can never be exact since every situation is uniquely different from any other previous experience we have had. However, based on the rough fit we form an understanding of what is happening in the now. Hence we look for similar patterns ignoring the 'no-patterns' since we don't have any corresponding images of 'no-patterns'.

Clearly the danger lies in leaving out portions of the present context for which we don't have any relevant or closely matching images in our stores. Therefore, we inadvertently leave out portions we don't understand thereby failing to have a complete understanding of the whole. The gaps between patterns and no-patterns, so essential to generate new knowledge, are left blank. So, it is easy to see how our closely held knowledge becomes part of our ignorance in any given situation.

Now when something goes wrong we start looking back to find out what went wrong or why something went wrong. And what do we try to do? We start examining the events or thoughts that went before it. It is something like using a mirror to trace back our thoughts that created the present problem or situation. We take this to be a linear path. But hold on. Did the images line up in a linear fashion? No not at all. We just plucked them off from different portions of the brain and imposed them on existing contextual situations to make sense of 'apparent' reality by matching a sensed pattern. So we try to travel down the thought line to get to the root of a problem that lies in the past—a construct of the mind. In doing so we are again tied down to the past because we simply don't have the images that match the gaps between patterns and no-patterns. We simply did not care to delve into the gap at all. The absence of knowledge of the gap is what creates all problems that we face.

The third way by which we are tied to the past is when we think forward from where we are now. That is when we leap into the future. How do we do that? We again take help of the previous knowledge and our rough incomplete understanding of the present context and then try to select sets of images that come up in our minds, put them together to frame a possible picture of the future. This is mostly what we understand by imagining (can be done more constructively). We then evaluate the imagined future with reference to the previous knowledge we have stored. Again we inadvertently ignore the gap that would always be present. Think of the confusion that would occur when someone imagines and someone else evaluates (as it usually happens) or think of communicating your imagined story to another person. The two persons having two distinct sets of images in their minds would not be communicating at all. One wouldn't understand what the other talks about. It would turn out to be like the Tower of Babel, which I suspect is really what the Biblical story stood for.

I find it extremely funny. Whether we try to make sense of the present or try to find a root cause or start imagining the future we are in some way or the other bonded to our past thoughts that effectively imprison us.

An Experiment

Now, imagine for a moment riding a thought wave (conceding for the moment linearity of a thought wave) being surrounded by a big spherical space with mirrors fitted all over the inner walls of such a space (an idea of our mental prison with reflecting surfaces that reflect the thoughts as it reaches the surface). Can we ever reach and break the wall and go beyond it? You know the answer. However, hard we might try we would never ever able to penetrate and go beyond the prison walls. Thoughts of the past are bounded by time and space and can't escape the limited dimensions of space and time.

This is exactly what is happening to us. When we examine a present context we unconsciously use the reflected images of the past. When we examine the cause of a problem we start off by bouncing off the reflected surface in our attempt to follow the old thought wave trying to go back in time. When we imagine the future we again use the reflected images to build up the future image which is unlikely to match the images formed in others minds (similar spherical spaces of others) or match the present context that we try to examine.

So, we are badly trapped irrespective of whether we think about the present, past or future. We even feel trapped while communicating our thoughts and ideas to others living in similarly separate worlds of their own. Then what might be the way out of such traps and mental prisons we created?

The secret then is to observe the present as it is. Good clear multisensory **Observation** is the starting point of the whole thing. We see patterns and no-patterns and the gap that exists between them. The challenge is to observe without any coloring of the past and consciously avoid false reflections of it. The next step is to **question** about what we are observing.

Questions may be like:

Is the system in equilibrium or far removed from equilibrium?

Is it oscillating, dissipating or wearing out?

What are the visible and the invisible parts?

What elements are involved?

How many planes of existence do we notice?

What changes in the relationships are happening?

What is being negated?

What are the authentic and inauthentic constraints at play?

What is growing or dying or being negated?

What direction the system is trying to take?

What is the natural tendency of the system?

Questions like these lead to probable answers that may be **tested** and **reflected** upon in a rational manner or lead to further questions and answers. We then **link** together the pieces of answers based on our observations (**serendipity**) to gain **insights** of the present context. Once such insights are obtained it is not difficult to understand the reality more completely as a whole, find reasons for our present problems and also **imagine** future outcomes, actions and scenarios. We are now in a position to communicate our insights in a logical and rational manner to any other rational person through **storytelling** to initiate meaningful actions to bring about effective long term changes.

So, to break free of our thought prison the steps involved are the following:

1. Uncolored multisensory Observation
2. Deep Questioning
3. Testing or Reflecting
4. Linking/serendipity
5. Insights of the present reality in its right context
6. Imagination to bring about changes
7. Storytelling

8. Actions to be implemented that are right for a given context.

This method of enquiry and learning might be called as **Observation Based Learning (OBL)**.

What are the advantages?

1. Break free of the past. Once done we allow ourselves to live in the flow of the now.
2. Learn to perpetually reinvent ourselves.
3. Proper contextual understanding of emergent complexity, patterns and apparent chaos.
4. Contribute to collective intelligence and wisdom through story telling.
5. Helps a person gain any amount of tacit & explicit knowledge in any field of human activity.
6. Gain the ability to employ insightful intelligence applicable to any situation.
7. Communicate without confusion or fear & be in the flow by focusing on the 'gap'.
8. Develop personal freshness and authenticity
9. Accelerates learning from anything going around us; even from casual conversations.
10. No need to change or challenge existing mental models that differ from person to person. Celebrate diversity and difference in experience. In light of new evidences and/or direct experiences the previously held models get changed or modified to give rise to new knowledge and models, ready to be shed with another unique experience.

These are big advantages to us and to the world at large since the principal constraint in any sustainable economy is the expression of authentic creativity; its development & nourishment and most importantly getting rid rid of what holds us back.

And none can take that freedom away—the freedom that comes from the new way of seeing and experiencing the world.

Chapter 29

Back to Mr. Giri's story

Acknowledging and accepting failure is a fundamental part of how businesses operate. In our case, it has ironically enabled our ability to grow and innovate quickly. I'm proud to say we have a culture that accepts embraces, and occasionally chuckles at failure.—Jeff Stibel Chairman & CEO, Dun & Bradstreet Credibility Corp.

In manufacturing industries the study of **Quality** and its improvement is a sixty year old story that started with Deming, Juran, Crosby and other legends who created the concept of Quality and its management.

The basic theme of Quality **Management** is about eliminating '**variations**' by keeping them under statistical control. So efforts are made to find special or general causes of variations and then find ways to either eliminate those undesirable variations by keeping them under an acceptable threshold limit. The fundamental approach to do so was statistical in nature that involves various statistical tools and techniques. And the general accepted framework was Deming's famous PDCA (Plan Do Check Act) cycle adopted and made popular by the Japanese.

Soon these ideas of variations spilled over to other fields like safety, risk and its assessment and even in management of organizations and fair to say to human societies under diverse cultural settings. Eliminate variation was the war cry. It was a world view of Statistical and Probabilistic understanding.

Since **Nemetics** takes a **Dynamical** view (fundamentally an energy view) of the interconnected and interdependent world its approach to Quality, Risks Productivity and Performance is rather different to that of the traditional statistical viewpoint. In other words Nemetics seeks to apply the concepts of Dynamics (especially Non-Linear Dynamics, Chaos and Complexity) from a practical point of view, which incidentally forms one of the unexplored or hardly explored **frontiers** of Non-linear Dynamics ('here lies dragons'—as early cartographers used to write on their maps). The underlying theme of Nemetical study is the play of waves and their connectedness or coupling to one another.

This is one fundamental part of Nemetics. The other fundamental part of Nemetics is to generate 'self awareness' in persons engaged in the dynamic process. With self awareness there is no need to cling to established models and theories. Any self aware person, who develops the ability to have a clear mind, can improve on anything by playing on the strengths of the system and reducing or eliminating weaknesses or imperfections inherent in the system. This process of developing self awareness starts with the observation or noticing or seeing things as they really are.

Our friend, Mr. Giri, along with few of his colleagues, was exposed to these two fundamentals and over a few months developed reasonable competence in self awareness and seeing the dynamical nature of any phenomenon.

Slowly, in a collective manner they started applying their new found competence to their problems and issues and engaged in their journey of deep observation based learning (OBL).

When they noticed at the physical level they saw how things are connected to one another and how changes cascaded through the system. They also saw the 'invisible' imperfections, which when corrected, changed the performance of the system. They made those small changes with the minimum effort, time and resources.

Then they noticed at the energy level and saw how energy was either lost or gained through various 'invisible' interfaces, which forced the system to go out of energy balance to create various problems. They corrected those to change the performance of the system.

After that they noticed the issues that were holding them back at the mental level. This was the hardest thing to do. At times it meant challenging their thoughts, ideas, assumptions, concepts, theories and working. But with patience and perseverance they saw most of it and discriminated between the useful and the worthless. With management backing they slowly eliminated the imperfections existing at the mental level. This was the most painful and slow process.

Next they looked at the wisdom level. The goals were to sustain their deep learning into easily recognizable patterns and continue learning faster. This was done with two aims in mind. First, was to communicate to others in the simplest possible ways. Second, was to make things noticeable for others to learn and act fast enough to sustain the performance of the system and improve the resilience of the system.

With all that smart and dedicated work in place the rewarding performance spoke for their work,

1. Performance shot up from 200 units per day to 2000 units per day from the same machines.
2. Quality rejection dropped from an average of 12 to 14% to around 5%.
3. They crossed the target of producing 8000 tons per month, which was earlier thought to be the productive limit of the system.

The collaborative effort of the small group was indeed a brilliant confirmation of what Margaret Mead said, "A small group of thoughtful people could change the world. Indeed, it is the only thing that ever has."

Chapter 30

Faith, hope & charity

I found these words of wisdom of Elie Wiesel, a holocaust survivor and a Nobel Peace Laureate. He states:

"The opposite of love is not hate, it is indifference.

The opposite of art is not ugliness, it is indifference.

The opposite of faith is not heresy, it is indifference.

And the opposite of life is not death; it is indifference between life and death."

I agree.

It boils down to notice or not; engage or not; mull or not; exchange or not. We have choices that create substantial differences in what we choose to manifest in our lives.

Much of what happens or would happen in our lives depends on our ability to concentrate our thought waves with patience and persistence triggered by the very act of observation/noticing/awareness (call it what you will).

If we were to sum up all of human spiritual understanding it would be Observation/Notice/Awareness (all three meaning the same). What we chose to manifest depends on the level of concentration we impart to our thoughts. And the level of concentration depends on our quality of observation.

However, our thoughts can be pessimistic or positive.

With pessimistic thoughts about the future, fear dominates. And with pessimistic thoughts about the past, which is self afflicting, shame comes uninvited only to manifest in reality.

But what can be said about productive actions; actions that create and preserve value? Productive actions are strengthened by Faith. Such actions can't be brought into reality without patience and persistence, which is born out of Hope. However, the purity of the intention (Charity) remains the guiding light throughout—from reality to new learning to new actions to new manifestation.

Hence "Faith must be placed on self aware observation", where opposite of faith is indifference ('notice not').

Hope lies in the quality of discernment. With right discernment only, we can afford to be patient and persistent; else not. Charity in actions/design is born out of authentic and pure intentions for free exchange of knowledge, learning and resources, else it doesn't help anyone.

To conclude:

a)   Faith in observation.
b)   Hope in discernment.
c)   Charity in actions/design.

EPILOGUE

'No Value' to Priceless

When someone says, 'This is what I think', it has no **value**.

When someone says, 'This is what I have seen', it has **little value**.

When someone says, 'This is what I have seen and it means this and that', it has **some value**

When someone says, 'This is what I have seen and this or that theory points out why it happens like that', it has **great value**.

When someone says, 'This is what I have seen and these I thought were the components of the system, which interacts in this particular way to produce what I saw', it has **immense value**.

But when someone says, 'This is what I have seen but I don't know why this happens the way it happens but we can all attentively see our own thoughts to find out why', it is **priceless**.

It is the ultimate expression of a self aware person who is ready to drop all concepts, notions, beliefs, theories and models to see reality as it is respecting diversity of views born of diverse experiences.

Once someone is self aware there are so many ways of noticing opportunities that lie right in front of our senses, waiting to help us win anywhere in the world!

Winning is about being deeply engaged in metanoia.

Wish you luck!

REFERENCES

1. Fifth Discipline Fieldbook, Senge, et al.

2. New Testament, King James Version.

3. Einstein & Tagore dialogue: http://www.brainpickings.org/index.php/2012/04/27/when-einstein-met-tagore/

4 Meaning of Art by Rabindranath Tagore

5. Patanjali Yoga Sutras

ABOUT THE AUTHOR

Dibyendu's passion is to solve complex, nagging organizational problems through minimal design interventions that give organizations ongoing benefits for years.

With 33 years of experience as improvement specialist/consultant he has guided more than 50 organizations to re-strategize through minimal design interventions to stay relevant in today's fast moving turbulent world.

He is an international authority on minimal Design Intervention, Maintenance, Maintainability, Manufacturing Strategy, Innovation and Entrepreneurship. He is the Chief Mentor of The International Nemetics Institute (TINI), Kolkata.

He lives in Kolkata with his wife and two sons. He loves yoga, meditation, painting, haikus, stories, listening to birds, watching fishes in the pond and enjoys long walks with his dog Clucky.

He may be contacted @Predictswan

ABOUT THE AUTHOR

Dibyendu's passion is to solve complex, nagging organizational problems through minimal design interventions that give organizations ongoing benefits for years.

With 33 years of experience as improvement specialist/consultant he has guided more than 50 organizations to re-strategize through minimal design interventions to stay relevant in today's fast moving turbulent world.

He is an international authority on minimal Design Intervention, Maintenance, Maintainability, Manufacturing Strategy, Innovation and Entrepreneurship. He is the Chief Mentor of The International Nemetics Institute (TINI), Kolkata.

He lives in Kolkata with his wife and two sons. He loves yoga, meditation, painting, haikus, stories, listening to birds, watching fishes in the pond and enjoys long walks with his dog Clucky.

He may be contacted @Predictswan